The Alcohol Escape Plan: A Little Book of Practical Advice from a Former Alcoholic

By Craig Beck

Dedicated to the memory of Denise Beck.

1967-2017

www.craigbeck.com
www.StopDrinkingExpert.com

DISCLAIMER AND TERMS OF USE AGREEMENT

Download the free companion tools for this book at
www.StopDrinkingExpert.com

Introduction

When alcohol becomes a problem it can create what is known as a double bind. Alcohol is making you miserable and destroying your life but you can't imagine life without it.

You may wonder how you will relax without your daily tipple. How will you have fun and be sociable without alcohol?

There are lots of worries and questions for the drinker considering quitting alcohol for good. The Alcohol Escape plan deals with many of the most common questions and concerns for the newly sober (or those planning to quit drinking but don't know how).

Craig Beck, a former problem drinker and bestselling author of 'Alcohol Lied to Me' deals with all the essential areas of life that are going to change when you kick alcohol into touch.

After giving up drinking himself, Craig has helped over 50,000 people to also stop drinking. Working with so many addicts over the years has given him a clear insight into the common worries.

Using the secrets of this book you can make quitting drinking a quick, easy and painless process.

Including:

- How do you have fun without alcohol?
- Dealing with your old drinking buddies.
- Can you ever go back to social drinking?
- How to deal with alcohol relapse?
- How you get the mindset to quit drinking and stay quit?
- How to reverse liver damage

- How to avoid drinking when life gets bad?

And much more.

How to Use This Book

For nearly two decades I was hopelessly addicted to alcohol. It was the thing that made me happy and it was the thing that made me miserable. I hated it every morning when I blinked open my bloodshot eyes and realized I had done it again. Instead of spending time with my family and loved ones I chose instead to drink myself into a coma and fall into bed at 8pm.

I was miserable, fat and tired – every morning was the same. I would drag myself to work feeling ashamed of myself, and vowing never to drink again. Then come 6pm, no sooner had I got home and taken my coat off had the wine been opened and poured. The cycle began again at 6pm everyday.

Alcohol was stealing everything good from my life. My marriage was going down the drain, I was too tired to play with my kids, my career was stagnating and I was running up a huge credit card debt because I spending all my disposable income on booze.

When I stopped drinking I sat down and worked out how much I had been spending on booze. It's no surprise to me now that I didn't conduct this exercise while I was still drinking. I simply didn't want to hear the financial cost of my habit. I didn't want to hear any negatives about booze (this is pure ostrich syndrome), the same technique that stopped me going to the doctor because I was afraid he would tell me to stop drinking.

Western society acts as though alcohol is nothing more than a social pleasantry to be enjoyed with friends, but in reality it is a drug so powerful it can even prevent intelligent individuals from getting urgent medical help. Make no bones about it; this is a very dangerous and sinister drug – the ultimate wolf in sheep's clothing!

At the peak of my drinking I was knocking back two bottles of wine a night, plus a bottle of whiskey over the weekend. At a rough guess that equates to a daily spend on alcohol of $23.00 per day. A weekly spend of $161.00 or $724.00 every month. Wow! No wonder I didn't want to see this figure while I was still drinking, that would have shocked and depressed me – BUT, it still wouldn't have stopped me drinking, and that is perhaps the scariest thought of all.

If I hadn't stopped drinking, it's entirely likely I would have continued consuming booze at that ungodly rate, or even increased it further to compensate for my growing tolerance to the effects of the drug. This means that over the next decade (if I had lived that long) I would have blown $86,940 on my addiction. Even this startling admission is only a half-truth, because it doesn't allow for any of those ridiculously priced $400 bottles of 'art', Christmas, Birthdays or any other formal excuse to get excessively drunk.

I was spending nearly $9000 a year on drinking a poison while telling my children and family that we couldn't afford the expensive vacations or other little luxuries that we might have actually been able to have if I wasn't lying to them, and of course, to myself. Hopefully, as you are starting to see, alcohol misled me. It lied to me, and it continues to lie to you – the challenge I throw down to you now is 'what are you going to do about it?"

I encourage you to honestly do this exercise for yourself and calculate how much money you are spending on a common drug addiction. You will no doubt come up with an amount of money, which you can think of a hundred different and better things to spend it on. Sadly the financial cost is almost insignificant when compared to the other factors that need to be considered when you try to take stock of what alcohol has stolen from you.

Booze affects everyone differently, but for me it made me sleepy. In a practical sense, what this meant for me is when I got home from work at let's say 6pm; the first glass of wine was poured by 6.05pm. Less than an hour later the first bottle was gone. By 8pm I had moved onto, and consumed about two thirds of the second bottle of wine (I would never drink the full second bottle because then I claim I had not drunk two full bottles of wine if anyone asked). At this point in the evening, after nearly two bottles of wine I could hardly keep my eyes open. I would spend the next 30 minutes staring at the clock wishing it were later so I could go to bed at a decent time. It would be rare for me to make it to 9pm, normally collapsing unconscious into bed between 8.30pm and 8.45pm.

I would sleep badly, waking several times to use the toilet and a few more times gasping for water to deal with the dehydration. My bloodshot eyes would blink open at 6am and I would head to work exhausted.

This was my life for longer than I care to admit, and while alcohol may not have the same outcome for you, there will almost certainly be another negative side effect to replace it. In my case, let's say a more reasonable bedtime for a 9 to 5 office worker is around 11pm. This means that my drinking took me offline for an additional 17 hours per week. Over ten years I spent 9,100 hours knocked out, unconscious because of my drug addiction. That time I will never get back, how many opportunities and experiences can you fit into nearly 10,000 hours?

The mind boggles.

The situation is even bleaker because I am a father; it's not just my time I was throwing away. Allow me to expand on this point to really ram home the gloomy message of what my drinking did:

If you are a parent I apologize for what I am about to ask you to do next. If you are visual or kinesthetic character type then this may be traumatic and painful for you to imagine, but please bear with me because I am doing this not to be cruel or give you nightmares, but rather to make a valuable point. Imagine for me; that tomorrow your child is abducted and you never see them again. Immediately such a horrific suggestion may remind you of what happened to the McCann family while on vacation in sunny Portugal a few years ago.

On Thursday 3rd May 2007, Jerry and Kate McCann put their little daughter Madeline to bed for the last time. At some point before midnight she was taken from her bed and has never been seen since.

If that happened to you and there was absolutely nothing you could do to prevent it happening, let me ask you, what price would you put on an hour spent with your daughter? If a few months later it were possible to buy the opportunity to see your child again and spend just one hour with them, what would you be prepared to pay?

Is it $1000, $10,000, $100,000 or is it priceless? Would you pay everything you had just to spend that one-hour with your child? I know for me the answer is the latter, and yet alcohol (the social drug) made me throw away over 9,000 hours that I could have spent with my lovely children Jordan and Aoife.

My children are the most precious things in my life, and yet a drug that people insist is just a bit of harmless fun, a beverage that they say is vital to the success of a party, a drink they demand must be consumed or you will be labeled boring and weird… Somehow this 'innocent' substance made me willingly give away 758 priceless days with my children.

I am going to take a break from writing at this point because I am so angry and feel so cheated that I don't think I can continue.

I will close this chapter by giving you one question to think about. What has alcohol stolen from you?

Is it your health, your time, your promotion, your money, your wife, your husband, your career? It may be one thing or it might be many, but as sure as night follows day, make no mistake about it… you are the victim of a serious theft. Unless you wake up and realize that the bottle of booze you thought was your friend is actually your worst enemy, then you will be a victim tomorrow, the day after and every day until the truth dawns on you.

The average drinker who joins my online stop drinking club is spending around $3000 a year on alcohol! That might sound a lot, and the tendency of any drinker is to assume they are nowhere near that amount. But $3000 is less than ten bucks a day and so if you are one of those people who drink a bottle of wine a day plus a bit more at the weekend then you are way over that figure. Let's keep the glass half full (excuse the pun) and we will stick with the average. Every person I have ever spoken to has agreed that they could find something important to do with $3000 dollars.

If I gave you that money today and told you to go blow it, what would you do with it?

- Maybe take the kids to Disneyland?
- Put it towards a new car?
- A romantic vacation?
- Put it towards the college fund?
- A medical bill or procedure?

- Pay off a credit card?

I knew that I could do so many amazing things for my family with that money and I tried to quit so many times that I lost count. Once I managed to go three months, until I decided that I was back in control and could safely have a glass of wine with my evening meal. With 48 hours I was back drinking as much as I ever had.

I had a eureka moment one day while driving home from work. I passed a runner in sweaty Lycra jogging in the wind and rain. As I stopped at a red light I watched this guy jog passed my car window and I though 'bloody idiot'. But as he got level with my line of sight I noticed that he didn't look miserable, quite the opposite – he looked like he was loving it! That's when I realized that people out there running in all weather conditions are not doing it because they are forcing themselves to do so. They are doing it because they enjoy it!

If I was going to successfully quit drinking I had to find a way to enjoy the process. Using willpower to deprive myself of something I loved was never going to work. I had to find a way to hate everything about alcohol so I could eliminate it from my life without the civil war of feeling like I am missing out on something.

I became a little bit OCD about discovering the truth about booze. I watched YouTube videos endlessly, I read medical journals, the Big Book and countless other addiction books. I examined the advertising around alcohol and worked out what emotional triggers the drinks companies were trying to tug on.

Then one day I got in from work and poured myself a large vodka and tonic. I looked at the drink and thought 'this will be the last drink I have'. The next day I woke up completely convinced that I was no longer a drinker… and I was right. That was my last drink!

I realized that I had unconsciously deconstructed my belief system around alcohol. I no longer saw benefits in drinking the stuff, I only saw the negatives. There was no longer civil war in my mind about this drug. I set about writing 'Alcohol Lied to Me' my account of how I had escaped the loop. I hoped it would help functioning alcoholics like me around the world, but I never dreamed it would become my fulltime job.

Since then I have helped over 50,000 people to quit drinking, exactly the same way I did all those years ago. While every drinkers believes his or her situation is unique, I have discovered that most people ask me exactly the same questions:

- How can I get to sleep without a drink?
- How do I have fun without alcohol?
- Why do people get upset when I won't drink with them?
- How can I go on vacation without having a drink?

The list goes on, but in this book I have picked the top 50 questions I get asked and answered them in full. My intention is you keep this book as your go to solution when a situation arises where you need a little extra guidance. I advise people to read it through in full at least once and then to keep it handy as your sobriety bible.

Perhaps not all the questions will apply to your situation but I still believe there is immense value in the cumulative absorption of the knowledge.

Why I started Stop Drinking Expert

The Stop Drinking Expert website and online alcohol addiction program came about because of the success of my book 'Alcohol Lied to Me'. The number of people who it helped shocked and surprised me.

I wrote the book with little expectation that it would one day become what I do for a living on a day-to-day basis. I simply wanted to share what had worked for me, in the hope that it may help other people in a similar situation with their use of alcohol.

I wasted a decade of my life trying to moderate my drinking. Despite the fact that alcohol was making me miserable and stealing everything that mattered, I still couldn't imagine my life without it. Some of the things I tried were dangerous (such as prescription only medication bought on the internet because no GP would prescribe it). Some things I tried were sensible (but fundamentally flawed) and some attempts to control my drinking were just downright silly.

The first time I went to see a GP and confess that I was worried about my drinking I was shocked by how hopelessly useless he was.

I remember, I had finally plucked up the courage to go and ask for help and instead of being given a solution I was offered a useless platitude. The doctor listened to my problem and do you know what he said in response to my admission of just how much I was drinking? He said 'yes, that is quite a lot. You should definitely try and reduce that'.

That was it! Apart from a vague suggestion that if I need any help I should come back. Did he not know how many times I had tried to make that appointment? Did he have no understanding of how out of control I felt?

I went home and opened a bottle of wine and pushed the whole issue to the back of my mind. His terrible approach to my cry for help had also given me permission to carry on doing what I was doing. Now I could drink and say 'well I tired to get help'!

It would be another six months of heavy drinking before I would address the issue again. I had a medical booked through the benefits package I had at work. Once again I decided to ask for help with my drinking.

On the day of my medical I pulled up at the hospital and it took me ten minutes to summon the courage to get out of the car. I eventually, nervously walking into the reception and gave my name. After I had been weighed and had my blood pressure checked by the nurse. I was shown through to the Doctor's office for something I was told was nothing more than a lifestyle chat. It sounded painless enough so I took the opportunity to explain that I was drinking far too much. I told the doctor that I was turning to alcohol to help deal with the stress of life more and more.

He listened carefully and nodded in agreement at various points. After I had finished baring my soul to him, he laughed.

He laughed!

He looked me in the eye and said "My good man, your drinking isn't a million miles away from my own. Try not to worry about it, just cut down a little".

Yet again I had used up every ounce of my resolve to reveal my deepest darkest fear to a stranger and yet again I was brushed off with banality. I left the hospital beyond depressed. I was now terrified, because if the medical profession couldn't help me then who on earth could?

For a long time I felt entirely trapped, I didn't want to go to Alcoholics Anonymous because I was a respected local businessman. I was the director of two companies and the patron of a large children's charity at this point. My reputation mattered to me! Nobody knew about my drinking problem, because it in no way affected my work or personal obligations.

I never missed a day of work through alcohol and my driving license was free of DUI's

I was trapped in an unbreakable loop, or so it seemed. I was drinking everyday as a matter of routine. This was even commonplace during times that I could describe as life as going well. However, when I hit a speed bump in the road, such as stress at work or family illness I would hit the hard stuff in a big way.

I couldn't deal with life anymore without alcohol to blur the edges of it.

When the drinking started to affect my health and I was seeing medical consultants because of the now constant pain in my right side – I knew I had to do something different. Everything I had tried had failed and failed dramatically. Each attempt to moderate my drinking had resulted in my drinking even more than before. I wasn't getting better, I was getting worse!

Alcohol is so powerfully effective at what it does because of the extremely slow way that it invades the life of the drinker. You can get hooked on heroin in a couple of weeks but alcohol takes years, sometimes even decades.

Because it moves so deliberately, we are like the frog that is dropped into a pan of cold water on the stove and slowly boiled to death.

I knew by this point that I could not moderate or stop my drinking by using willpower, gimmicks or medication. I had tried every combination of that over the past few years – nothing had worked. I fell back on my training in hypnotherapy and Neuro Linguistic Programming. I knew that I had to frame alcohol differently.

Instead of seeing it as a benefit in my life, I had to flip alcohol around so it became as abhorrent to me as heroin and other drugs. Over next few months I became obsessed with alcohol, not in the same way I had previously. Now I was OCD about discovering the truth behind the smoke and mirrors of the glossy marketing.

One by one I took everything I believed about booze deconstructed it and instead learnt the truth. I slowly understood why we think alcohol helps us relax, be more sociable, feel more confident and the hundreds of other lies that the drug has successfully woven into the daily fabric of life.

One day I bought a bottle of vodka and I sat alone staring at it. I poured a large glass and drank it. As I swallowed it I became aware that I was not enjoying it at all. I knew instantly that it would be my last day as a drinker.

The next morning I woke up and poured the remaining vodka down the kitchen sink. I felt free but more than that, I felt peaceful. Previously when I had stopped drinking there was always a sensation of panic at the back of my mind. I would worry whether I could 'do this' and would a life without alcohol even be worth living. This time I felt calm and confident – I knew that I didn't want alcohol in my life any more.

A few weeks later I started to write the book 'Alcohol Lied to Me', I still felt my situation was unique but I hoped it might help a few people out of the trap.

It wasn't until about a year later that I started getting a regular flow of emails from people saying the book had changed their life. They were grateful but were asking lots of the same sorts of questions. I realized then that I could help a lot more people if I built something online. A resource that was always there to help people who had been addicted to alcohol.

This is how the Stop Drinking Expert was born and I am very proud to have helped over 50,000 drinkers escape the loop of alcoholism and find their own happy sober solution.

If this book is your first step into sobriety may I suggest you instead start with Alcohol Lied to Me. That book is the foundation of your new mindset. As I mentioned this book has been compiled from my many years of helping people to stay quit.

The Alcohol Escape Plan is a powerful weapon in your arsenal and congratulations on taking a step that most people will never do.

Why do you refer to alcohol as the Evil Clown?

"I mean, that's at least in part why I ingested chemical waste - it was a kind of desire to abbreviate myself. To present the CliffNotes of the emotional me, as opposed to the twelve-column read.

I used to refer to my drug use as putting the monster in the box. I wanted to be less, so I took more - simple as that. Anyway, I eventually decided that the reason Dr. Stone had told me I was hypomanic was that he wanted to put me on medication instead of actually treating me. So I did the only rational thing I could do in the face of such as insult - I stopped talking to Stone, flew back to New York, and married Paul Simon a week later." — Carrie Fisher

It may seem slightly schizophrenic to suggest that you and your addiction are two separate things. However, in my many years of dealing with alcohol addicted individuals I have never once concluded that the person in question is 'broken', 'weak' or 'just plain stupid'.

In actual fact I have noticed that alcohol seems to pray particularly on the intelligent and introverted more than most. Brainpower, creative thinking and introversion are all a curse as much as they are a gift. If an individual manages to harness and focus this state of mind they can achieve truly breathtaking things. However, if left without boundaries and direction it can make a person beyond miserable.

Uncontrolled introversion can lead to chronic overthinking, depression, worry, anxiety and panic. When someone like this discovers alcohol the Evil Clown really sits up and pays attention. The clown knows that these people need to be nurtured and cared for because they are easy to hook into the drug.

Alcohol gives us over thinkers a tool to stop the craziness of our minds for a brief moment. If alcohol wasn't hell bent on destroying every aspect of our lives, some might be able to claim it's a worthwhile tool. However, that's a bit like saying rain would be great if it didn't get you wet. The Evil Clown wants these people dead and he will stop at nothing until he gets this result.

At the moment it probably doesn't make a great deal of sense that there is a third party living inside you. But let me explain how I know this to be true.

When you develop a drink problem you are acutely aware of just how much damage is being done to your life. Everything that ever mattered to you is under violent attack. Your finances are crashing, your relationships are dying, your career is treading water (at best) and your health is starting to fail. Yet, despite everything falling down around you, there is still a voice in your head that says 'what you need to deal with this is a drink'.

This is quite clearly an insane viewpoint. It would be like going to hospital with cancer and the doctor suggesting they are going to try and cure the problem by giving you more cancer. However, nobody I ever met in my member's area is clinically insane. So where does this unhinged view come from?

The Evil Clown

99.9% of your brain is beautiful, powerful and capable of creating amazing things in your life. However, buried deep in the middle is the Evil Clown. He is small but noisy. Let me prove that he is there:

Stop reading for a moment and sit quietly for a few moments. Next I want you to vividly imagine never being allowed to have another alcoholic drink again for the rest of your life.

Most drinkers will feel a sensation of panic, fear and denial. They feel all these counter intuitive sensations despite how desperate they are to quit drinking. This insane noise is the Clown screaming in horror.

He doesn't' usually lose his cool like that. The Evil Clown is clever; he can generally control his temper. He can for the most part keep the smile painted on his face and whisper nicely in your ear. He is a master manipulator and like all control freaks he will do what it takes to get the outcome he wants.

My daughter is a ninja of this sort of persuasion technology. If she wants something she doesn't just ask for it (like my son would do). She will tell me how much she loves me, how much of a great Dad I am and how lucky she feels to have me in her life… then and only then she will drop the bomb. "Dad, you know how my sneakers are looking a little old now. Would you mind buying me some more at the Mall today?'

When you get home after a hard day at work, the Evil Clown wants you straight onto the drug. Alcohol gives him power and control. However, despite how much he wants to, he doesn't just scream 'drink alcohol you asshole' in your ear. Instead he acts like my daughter does when she wants some new sneakers. He gently whispers in your inner ear. He tells you how great you are that you got through such a tough day. He tells you that you deserve to let off some steam and really kick back. Have a drink and relax my friend, it's about time you did something for yourself.

He doesn't need to keep this performance up for long, he knows the moment you take the first sip he has you. The drug will do the rest, he can go back to bed and leave you to it.

Have you noticed that you sometimes let out a beautifully deep outward sigh when you take your first drink of the day? But you never do it with the second drink. This is the Evil Clown screaming in ecstasy that yet again he tricked you, and so easily too.

At first this concept may feel scary but there is some very good news. The Clown can't survive unless you feed him. He has no way of nourishing himself and unless you provide for him he will quickly lose power and eventually fall into a deep coma. You will notice I didn't say die! The Evil Clown can never die. One glass of alcohol at anytime will act like a heart defibrillator, violently slamming him back into the waking world.

No, you can't kill him but you can easily sentence him to a lifetime in a tiny prison cell. And for the sort of crimes this twisted malevolent demon has committed there can be no more fitting place for him to rot away his time.

Whose Fault Is it?

At the end of the day, you are solely responsible for your success and your failure. And the sooner you realize that, you accept that, and integrate that into your work ethic, you will start being successful. As long as you blame others for the reason you aren't where you want to be, you will always be a failure. Erin Cummings

There is no arguing the fact; problems with alcohol can make you downright miserable. It can feel like being trapped inside an endless loop. You keep running, hoping against hope to find the exit but the same story just keeps repeating over and over. It all feels very much like the background scenery in a 'Scooby Do' cartoon.

Society is a little bit twisted when it comes to alcohol addiction. People tend to approach addicted drinkers with pity, as though they are strange broken people. We don't treat smokers the same way. If someone told you they were addicted to nicotine, you would be highly unlikely to pour on the sympathy and declare how terrible it must be for them.

Because of this kink in our collective perception it is very easy to feel sorry for ourselves. We can even avoid responsibility entirely by insisting that we have a disease called 'alcoholism'. Almost as though something terribly unfortunate happened to us. However, this sort of pity party solves nothing and serves no purpose.

If you do join my online stop drinking program you will quickly discover that I am not the sort of therapist that is going to hold your hand and tell you how terrible it is for you.

Alcohol addiction is a miserable affliction and we can choose to blame our parents, the marketing, the social conditioning or any number of explanations. But this sort of thinking and rationalizing will only delay and hinder your way out of the maze.

In the members area of the Stop Drinking Expert there are people who have been sober for years. There are also people who still can't go more than a day without a drinking. If you ask me what the difference is between the two types of people, I would say: The sober people are willing to do all the things that the drinkers refuse to do.

People who are firmly committed to sobriety don't have excuses, only the drinkers do. Show me someone who is still drinking and I guarantee you that they have a list of pre-prepared reasons why they can't stop yet! They will tell you that 'they are having a tough time at home/work at the moment', 'they will just get Christmas out of the way', 'as soon as the vacation is done and dusted' etc. The list of reasons to fail goes on and on.

Your journey to escaping alcoholism begins with a flat refusal to give yourself permission to fail and taking 100% responsibility for the situation you find yourself in. Notice I did not use the word 'blame'. Blame in any situation is the pointless bleating of the ego and nothing more. Blame never serves any worthwhile purpose. NEVER!

For example, let's say your goal is to run the 4-minute mile. Unfortunately during training one day you fall and break your leg. You may think that this is a really great reason to explain why you have failed to achieve your goal, and perhaps it is. But does using the excuse give you anything in it's place? You didn't run the 4-minute mile and an excuse is no substitute for that. You missed your target, suck it up and deal with it. Stop using excuses to justify your failure.

Remember the Rocky quote… winning has nothing to do with how hard you can hit. It's about how hard you can get hit and keep getting back up. When you come up with an excuse you are choosing the stay down on the mat.

To become a happy sober person you take responsibility and develop an internal state of mind that takes ownership of the challenge. You must have a deep determination to deal with this problem no matter what is thrown at you. Not because someone else told you to or because you feel guilty about letting other people down but purely for the love of yourself.

Start by taking a pen and paper and sitting down alone. Write down every reason why you drinking alcohol. Common reasons include:

- Because it helps me relax
- I need it to cope with my stressful life
- I can't sleep without a drink
- It's my only pleasure
- It helps me be more sociable

Keep writing until you have exhausted yourself. Keep scribbling until every single reason you have for drinking is down there on that piece of paper. In The Alcohol Escape Plan you will find every excuse you can think of explained and deconstructed in full. I will give you the truth behind the bullshit, if you will forgive the expression.

Every single reason to drink, even if it seems entirely logical is nothing but an illusion – including that list I just gave you. There is a reason why alcohol is the second most addictive substance on planet earth (just behind heroin). That is because it is exceptionally good at what it does and it is remarkably good at making all it's traps and tricks look harmless and insignificant.

Alcohol hooks people in so slowly that you don't notice what is going on until it's too late. It's like falling into very thick and slow moving quicksand. The sand is so thick that for a while you are completely unaware that you are sinking at all. It feels very much like you are standing firmly on solid ground, and so you keep on walking. Alcohol will let you get all the way out into the middle before it starts to pull you under. Just like being in real quicksand, kicking and screaming and blaming someone else for not warning you won't help you get out. All it will do is accelerate the speed at which you sink.

Wake up and smell the coffee! You got yourself into this loop and it is you who is going to get yourself out. I challenge you to learn the truth about every one of those reasons to drink that you noted down. Dissect them and tear them apart until you fully understand how the illusion is being performed. Then accept 100% responsibility of dealing with this addiction.

There is no magic bullet out there; there is no pill you can take to make this go away. There is a solution but you can't buy it, because you already own it. It's inside you – your focus and commitment to get this poison out of your life at all costs is the secret to escaping the loop of alcohol addiction once and for all.

Does Alcohol Really Give You Confidence?

You gain strength, courage, and confidence by every experience in which you really stop to look fear in the face. You are able to say to yourself, 'I lived through this horror. I can take the next thing that comes along.' Eleanor Roosevelt

Does drinking make you more confident? There is a swift answer to this question…No! Alcohol really gives you stupidity, and there is a big difference between the two.

People *believe* that they feel more self-assured and confident when they have had a drink. There is even common parlance for it "Dutch Courage".

'It's one of those expressions we use without giving much thought to where it came from. In numerous ways, the Dutch used to be Britain's dearest neighbors. From the rise of the United Provinces throughout the sovereignty of Queen Elizabeth I and up until the eclipse of the Netherlands as a major power in the Napoleonic conflicts. They were sometimes enemies but more usually co-religionist allies, significant trading associates and irregular provincial rivals. Even more than that a Dutchman, William, even went on to become king of England in 1689.

These connections between the two countries have forced the word "Dutch" to appear repeatedly in the English language. Slang dictionaries have plenty of phrases such as 'going Dutch', 'Dutch auction', 'Dutch uncle' and of course "Dutch Courage".

'Dutch courage' has a pair of possible origins. The first derives from the denigrating idea that *Johnny Foreigner is a weaker chap that the firm and sturdy Englishman.* Whether this bounder was cruising up the Medway or facing down the locals in the East Indies, he required a handful of drinks before a battle.

The second idea relates more directly to the use of a specific alcoholic beverage "gin" to bolster one's "confidence or bravery" in battle.

Gin in its contemporary form, was reputedly invented by the Dutch physician Franz de le Boë in the 17th century. British troops fighting Louis XIV together with their allies in the Low Countries appreciated the calming influences of Dutch gin before heading into battle.

Whether it expressly referred to gin, 'Dutch courage' as an English colloquialism tended to mean using spirits, not just beer, to reinforce self-belief.

This all sounds very poetic and romantic, but the real story is less so. Front line soldiers in these sorts of battles were really nothing more than cannon fodder. They were considered the affordable and expendable casualties of war. They were the poor sods that would charge into the first and most gruesome line of defense while the opulent generals sat at a safe distance on handsome stallions looking on.

However, willingly charging toward your gruesome dismemberment and eventual death 'doesn't so much need bravery or confidence. 'What's needed is a good dose of stupidity and poor decision-making. It just so happens that alcohol is perfect for inducing both these mental states in a person. Booze was the ultimate tool to manipulate men to die for their country.

'Here's the hard reality. One of the reasons why alcohol is so good at what it does (successfully killing someone every minute or every day). Is because they very first thing the drug does is disable the section of the brain responsible for making sound decisions. This is why people find it so hard to have just one drink and then stop. While sober, you have the seemingly unbreakable determination just to have one little drink. However, as soon as the drug plays its first hand, you become as weak and vulnerable as a newborn baby.

This effect on the logic areas of the brain is also the reason why people become less risk-averse after drinking.

Becoming less able to gauge risk does not make you confident it makes you stupid. So yes, you may have had the "nerve" to approach the hot girl after you had had a drink but 'don't kid yourself that you were acting bravely or even more confidently.

No beautiful woman ever looks at a drunk man, who is clumsily trying to pick her up and thinks "wow he is so confident". The inebriated chump who firmly believes he can jump from one hotel balcony to the next, is not being super confident.

There is no such thing as Dutch Courage. Alcohol makes you stupid. I would argue that in most of the occasions where alcohol is used for so-called Dutch Courage. For example, making a presentation at work, going for a job interview, talking to a man or woman you are attracted to, etc. Perhaps deliberately making yourself progressively less intelligent is about the worst possible choice you could make.

'Don't you agree?

How do you have fun without alcohol?

"Fun is one of the most important - and underrated - ingredients in any successful venture. If you're not having fun, then it's probably time to call it quits and try something else", Richard Branson

Drinkers can't imagine going to a party that doesn't feature alcohol. They will pre-decide that it will be boring and dull. Back when I was a drinker I would have point blank refused to attend a party that didn't have alcohol. My ex-wife was friendly with a couple that hardly drank alcohol at all. Perhaps once a year we would be invited around for a meal. I would bitch and moan like a petulant child. All the way through the meal I would sip the water and continually glance at my watch. Fifteen years later when I look back I can't remember anything about them, other than they stopped me drinking. They may have been the most lovely and amazing people who ever walked the earth – I will never know.

At the time I was 100% sure that I was right! You can't have fun without booze. However, the truth is it's not that alcohol makes a party but rather drinkers of alcohol are miserable when they can't get access to their drug. So it's not the party that's dull, it's the addict – who only knows how to be sociable if they are able to engage in consumption of their preferred drug.

At the height of my addiction I couldn't even go to watch a movie without first planning how I could also drink at the same time. I would even sneak a bottle of whiskey into the movie theatre with me. I would order a big gulp coke and mix it with Scotch so I could sip at my drug for the entire duration of the movie. Pathetic.

Alcohol doesn't enable fun, it prevents it! This has been demonstrated to me this weekend in the most profound and hard-hitting way. I live in Cyprus these days and my grown up children live in the United Kingdom. So I don't get to see them as often as I would like. This means that when we do spend time together we like to make it count.

This weekend I flew to London to have a weekend in the city with my daughter. We had an amazing time together; we went shopping, took in a west end show and spent seriously quality time together. I am so grateful that alcohol is no longer present in my life to steal these moments from me.

Alcohol is a thief! It steals your money, your health, your relationships and worst of all – your time. I spent over £100,000 on alcohol and while that is a crime, I can make more money! Time is the one thing you can never make more of.

If I were still drinking, this weekend would have been entirely different. Yes, I would have described it as 'more fun' but let me explain what a drinker's definition of 'more fun' really means.

We would have spent significantly less time doing what my daughter wanted to do. Lunch would have been in a pub and would have taken about 3 times as long. Afterwards I would feel a bit tired and suggest a lie down before we head out to see the show.

During the play I would be thinking about the interval, when I could have a drink. I would enjoy the show, as much as I could but it wouldn't have been the best part of the evening.

I would have woken up the next morning feeling terrible and full of guilt because the weekend was supposed to be about my daughter and yet again I made it about alcohol.

- In short, more fun means that I am here physically but not mentally.
- More fun means more selfish behavior from me.

- More fun means we will do less with the time we have.
- More fun means missing the whole point of the weekend.

How do you have fun without alcohol? That was the question that launched this chapter of the book but it's almost impossible to answer. The whole premise that alcohol creates fun is a house built on sand. There are no foundations to support the hypotheses.

If you are skeptical I can easily prove my theory to you. Just go to a party and be the only sober person there. You will be shocked at what you see unfold before your eyes.

Being the only sober person at a drunken party feels a little like being Neo in the Matrix. You are the only one aware that the 'crazy, fun world' being experienced by everyone else isn't real. The reality is much more sinister and scary than anyone is conscious of.

You will witnesses your intelligent and compassionate friends turning into bumbling, emotionally unstable zombies. You will sit with a bemused smile on your face, confused as to why everyone is laughing at a joke or incident that wasn't in the least bit funny. Slowly you will become aware that you are the only human being left in the room. Your friends have become nothing more than a bunch of chimpanzees on a sugar rush.

By the end of the night many people will no longer have the brain power to speak, some will fall over and hurt themselves (much to the amusement of the other primates) and some will black out and have to be carried to bed.

The next morning all your friends will wake up feeling like they want to die before heading to Facebook to wax lyrical about 'what an amazing night we had'. Everything about alcohol appears to be a little bit insane when viewed with sober eyes.

Your friends will tell you that they had an amazing night. But they will use words like 'slaughtered', 'smashed', 'wrecked' and 'wasted' to describe how they felt. They will look you straight in the eye and through their bloodshot, exhausted outlook say this to you with 100% conviction.

The question is not 'how do you have fun without alcohol', the truth is drinkers don't really understand what 'fun' is. Exactly the same way that people inside the Matrix refuse to accept that what they see isn't real.

You can't convince drinkers of this, so don't even try. You can't change other people; you can only change yourself and the way you respond to other people.

Why do people get upset when I don't drink?

"Your time is limited, so don't waste it living someone else's life. Don't be trapped by dogma - which is living with the results of other people's thinking. Don't let the noise of others' opinions drown out your own inner voice. And most important, have the courage to follow your heart and intuition", Steve Jobs

We live in a distorted reality where the regular consumption of a proven carcinogenic poison is considered normal. Conversely the people who don't want to drink to the poison are considered strange, unsociable and boring.

If aliens visited this planet from another world and observed this behavior they would think we were deranged.

Perhaps we are?

Actually people who don't have a problem with alcohol probably don't get upset when you refuse to drink with them, why would they? However, individuals who are also addicted to alcohol tend to respond aggressively. They automatically dislike anyone who refuses to proliferate the social proof that drinkers find so comforting.

The human body reacts to alcohol exactly as you would expect it to respond to the ingestion of any poison. It makes you feel ill, before eventually forcing you to vomit and expel the offending substance. No matter how defensive a drinker gets about his or her use of alcohol. At the back of their mind they instinctively know that one-day the habit must stop, one way or another.

The thought of this is terrifying to the addict and rather dealing with the painful issue head on he/she prefers to stick their head in the sand, ostrich style. Part of the way in which a drinker explains away the entirely illogical behavior of drinking poison for fun is to point out that everyone around them also drinks.

This is psychologically understandable. Social proof is a commonly used component of human decision-making. We tend to default to the position that other people around us know better than us. We will often follow the crowd even when we are sure that they are wrong. This has been proven in social experiments time and time again.

For example: A group of 20 individuals were told to examine three identical pieces of string and identify the one that was longer than the others.

However, only one of the individuals was a genuine participant in the experiment. The other members of the test had been instructed to look carefully at the identical pieces of string and confidently confirm that the third piece of string was longer than the others.

In nine out of ten cases the genuine participant, having watched twenty other people point to the third string, also went on to confirm that it was longer than the rest.

Drinkers use the social proof of other drinkers to ease their nagging doubts and worries about continually ingesting something that they know to be fundamentally harmful. So, when you come along and refuse to drink the poison you cause dramatic psychological pain to the other person. It is unlikely to be recognized by them on a conscious level but their aggression towards you is a direct response to the sensation of pain.

Anyone who has quit drinking and been on the receiving end of this sort of thing will confirm that 'aggression' is not too strong a word. I was once confronted at a Christmas party by a woman who claimed I was ruining the party for everyone, because I refused to drink.

I questioned how my choice of drink could have an impact on the fun of other people. This was a mistake, because trying to debate with drunk people is like trying to make an igloo in the desert... pointless!

She claimed that she couldn't fully relax and let her hair down because she was aware of me watching her and being judgmental. I am not sure where this insecurity came from but she looked pretty bloody relaxed to me already.

In my book 'Alcohol Lied to Me' I tell the story about my friend the airhostess who thought I was ill because I refused the free alcohol she was offering. I have also had male friends call me 'gay' because I refused a drink. How my choice of beverage has any bearing on my sexual preferences I will never know.

Human beings are motivated in all areas of life by only two forces. Firstly, the need to avoid pain and secondly the desire to achieve pleasure. When you decline an alcoholic beverage and indirectly cause this person psychological pain, they must respond in one of the two ways. Of course they could choose to also stop drinking and move towards pleasure. However, this is not the path of least resistance and so they are more likely to try and remove the pain, in this case you and or your behavior.

If the drinker can get you drinking then the social proof is restored and the pain will go away. If that fails they may just avoid you and ergo also avoid the pain your behavior is inflicting on them.

No matter what they say to you, no matter how offensive, manipulative, cajoling or personal they get – remember this is their problem and not yours. The process of stopping drinking without using willpower is one of slowly de-cloaking the dark magician and revealing the truth about the drug.

You can see this slowly happening with cigarette smoking. Not so long back cigarettes were seen as glamorous, sexy and a fundamental part of being sociable. More and more these day's smokers are banished to stand outside in the cold to take their drug. It is seen more as a dirty habit than a social activity. While smokers still have the social proof of other smokers they no longer have the approval of society as a whole.

Unfortunately the alcohol industry is about twenty to thirty years behind the cigarette industry. Booze manufactures are still allowed to advertise, and say pretty much anything they want. Their packaging is free of graphic warning labels and the product is freely available, not an under the counter item as cigarettes are increasingly becoming.

There is an incorrect assumption that cigarettes are more harmful than alcohol. The truth is nicotine is the sixth most addictive substance on earth. Alcohol is actually way ahead in second place, just behind heroin. We tend to see cigarettes and cigars as bad and booze as harmless. The truth is, alcohol kills someone every 60-90 seconds and it is this fact that drinkers don't like to be reminded about by teetotalers like you!

Stick to your guns (or cranberry juice) you are not the one doing something strange. The people who drink poison for fun are the ones out of whack with reality.

Is that pain in my side caused by alcohol?

"Money doesn't mean anything to me. I've made a lot of money, but I want to enjoy life and not stress myself building my bank account. I give lots away and live simply, mostly out of a suitcase in hotels. We all know that good health is much more important", Keanu Reeves

Do you have a dull ache in your right abdomen? If the answer to that question is yes then keep reading, I have some important information for you. If not you can skip this chapter if you prefer.

In *Alcohol Lied to Me* I told the story of how my drinking ended up putting me in hospital. I didn't go into too much detail because I thought the problem had been relatively unique to me. What I have since discovered from helping thousands of drinkers to also escape the trap of alcohol addiction is my symptoms are extremely commonplace in heavy drinkers. Perhaps my story resonates with you?

In January 1997 after a particularly heavy festive season, I started to get a dull ache in my right abdomen just under my right rib. I dismissed it as a hundred different minor, insignificant medical problems from a bit of food poisoning to an intolerance of wheat; I even considered paying £300 for a food allergy blood test. In summary, I considered everything apart from the obvious, that the 140 units of alcohol a week were destroying my insides the same way alcohol destroys all life at a cellular level.

In February 1997, the dull ache was preventing me getting to sleep and I started searching the Internet for my symptoms. As I scanned the possible reasons for a pain in this region I suddenly became genuinely scared. Website after website suggested liver cancer, liver failure, liver cirrhosis, pancreatic failure, alcohol induced gall bladder disease. The lists went on and on, all horrific illnesses, all caused by alcohol, and many were irreversible. I made an appointment to see my doctor.

In my lifetime I have never had anything seriously wrong with me; I have only ever been to the doctor for a cold or simple chest infection. My past experiences with the medical profession mean I always confidently expect to be told that the condition will clear up on its own, or that a short dose of antibiotics would be all that is needed. This time was different.

I sat in the doctor's waiting room, shaking with fear. I walked in and explained my symptoms. He asked how much I was drinking, I lied and said I used to drink a lot but now I have no more than a glass of wine a night. Can you believe that even at this point I still lied? Of course you can – you still do it all the time! This is the power of this drug we freely hand out to children at celebrations as a 'treat' to make them feel grown up.

In honest fear for my life, face to face with a medical professional who was there to help me, I still lied to protect my opportunity to drink. Despite the fact that it was slowly killing me, I couldn't cope with the possibility that it would be taken away from me, so I lied to the doctor.

If you are not from the United Kingdom, let me explain that doctors in England are normally seen at the cost of the state on the National Health Service. Doctor's surgeries are usually over-subscribed and getting an appointment is sometimes difficult. My allocated time with Doctor White was five minutes, behind me there were another seven patents all waiting for their own five minutes. After 35 minutes of examinations and questions, I knew this was going to be a very different experience than I was used to at the doctors.

I still expected, even after all the fuss, for the doctor to nod reassuringly and say "well, I've checked you over and you seem fine, come back in a month if it doesn't improve". Dr White had a concerned but kind face, he looked up from his notes over his small round glasses and said "there is a very real possibility there is something serious behind your pain. I don't have the facilities here to examine you to the level I need to, so I am having you sent to the gastroenterology department at the hospital".

Hospital! Surely not! That is where sick people go; the health service is overstretched as it is, surely they wouldn't waste a valuable bed on someone young and healthy like me? As I walked home, neither cured nor reassured, this was the point when I realized this was not a figment of my imagination. I had possibly seriously damaged my body by selfishly drinking my attractively packaged poison.

I sat at home and watched my children play, and it felt like my heart had been ripped out. Knowing how much I love my family, how could I do that to them?

How could I leave my children with out a daddy?

How could I be so selfish that I would make my children go through the pain of watching their dad's funeral?

How could I be so pathetic that I would risk making my wife a single parent, with two devastated children to look after and no income? I am not ashamed to tell you my world was ripped apart that evening, and I cried myself to sleep in a world of self-pity, regret and guilt.

Before, during and after my hospital visits I spent a lot of time on Google trying to prove that my health problems were not the result of my drinking. I wanted a 'get out of jail free' card that would allow me to continue drinking. I point blank did not want to accept the possibility that I had damaged myself with alcohol and worse than that I might have to quit drinking all together if I wanted any chance of recovery.

I would search for hours until I found a benign disease that roughly matched my symptoms. I diagnosed myself with dozens of different illnesses from simple muscles strains to irritable bowl syndrome. I was willing to consider everything and anything accept the most obvious and likely culprit.

This behavior is a well-documented behavioral pattern of human beings. It is called confirmation bias and has been proven time and time again to be the primary cause of many poor judgments. Essentially confirmation bias is the process of searching for evidence to back up your currently beliefs and then stopping when you find the 'proof' required to support your original position. We close our eyes to what we are doing and ignore the obvious fact that pretty much anything can be 'proved' with supporting evidence found online today.

For example if it is my profoundly held belief that ghosts exist then my online search criteria is likely to be looking for examples of past ghost sightings and not a more open minded and objective approach to the subject. Google being the giant that it is will no doubt furnish me with millions of websites to back up my beliefs and bingo I have my proof and because it doesn't make any waves in my current belief structure I am willing to overlook and ignore the blatant confirmation bias.

If you are routinely drinking alcohol to excess and you have a 'dull ache' in your right flank that may even be radiating around to your back then you need to stop drinking immediately and see a doctor. Pain or discomfort in this area of a problem drinker is likely to be associated with distress to the liver and or pancreas. You may be tempted to think that if it was a serious problem then the pain could not be described as a dull ache, surely you may postulate that serious damage would result in serious pain? In my particular case I could never honestly describe myself as being in pain but more that I was conscious that something was wrong.

For example I would always sleep on my left side because it was uncomfortable to lie on my right, it felt as though there was a hard lump in the mattress. Would you believe I even considered buying a new bed, despite the screamingly obvious fact that it was only comfortable when I lay on one particular side. How about that for confirmation bias?

The reason the mildness of the pain is not a reason for reassurance is down to the composition of the liver. This amazing organ is the most forgiving of the human body, if you treat it with respect it will filter the toxins out of your body and even repair itself when it gets damaged. Unless you drink poison for decades and then it gets to the point where it says 'enough is enough – I give in'. When your liver says 'I give in' that's it I am afraid, its game over you are a dead man or dead woman walking.

But wait Craig, I think you are being a little melodramatic there are you forgetting about liver transplants. No, my friend I have taken into consideration the possibility of a transplant and you are still done for. You are doomed by the math; by the time you realize you have destroyed your liver you will be given between three and six months to live. There are currently eighteen thousand people in the United States awaiting a liver transplant and the average wait time is around three hundred and thirty days, long after you are in the ground I am afraid.

The liver doesn't complain about the vast amount of abuse you are throwing at it because it contains virtually no nerve endings. The dull ache you feel is not coming from the liver, as it is unable to detect pain. However, as the liver becomes inflamed and swells and deforms it presses on other nearby sensitive organs in the abdomen.

If you are experiencing the dreaded drinkers dull ache it may mean that your liver is now so swollen that it is applying enough pressure on other parts of your body to cause you pain. I am telling you from experience, don't waste time trying to find an alternative explanation online and do not miss what might be your last chance to act before you do irreversible damage and become person 18,001 waiting for a liver that will never arrive.

Can an alcoholic ever go back to drinking in moderation?

"I think that the power is the principle. The principle of moving forward, as though you have the confidence to move forward, eventually gives you confidence when you look back and see what you've done." – Robert Downey Jr.

I know many readers would prefer to cut down rather than stop, but the only logical solution is for you to step out of the mousetrap and never get back in. If you are dependent upon alcohol and you don't want to stop, you have not quite grasped the problem. If a heroin addict came up to you and said "I have decided to only use drugs on a Tuesday and never any other day", how confident are you that if you bumped into him again in a years time that would be still the case. Alcoholism is a binary condition, it is either on or off, you can't be a little bit alcoholic in the same way you can't be a little bit pregnant!

You may need to read this book over and over before you get to this point and your decision is in harmony with my advice. Stopping completely really is the best option for you, but you must come to that decision on your own. You can't be convinced by me, your family or friends and nobody can order you to take this stance, it has to come deep from within you.

If you don't currently feel like that, if you are still at the point where you believe you can control the situation, or that you enjoy it too much to stop completely, don't panic or beat yourself up too much. You are not alone in this struggle. In my online community you will find people who are in exactly the same position as you. Nobody has ever developed a drink problem and then woke up the next morning and cured it in a eureka moment of perfection.

Part of the journey to sobriety is experiencing the futility of trying to find a way to keep the bits you like while removing the consequences you don't want. It is like trying to bail out the Titanic with a bucket; for a while you may believe you are making headway, but very soon you start to see that you can't possibly succeed. I tried dozens and dozens of different buckets before I came to the realization that the good parts of drinking go hand in hand with the bad, and you can't have one without the other.

Here are just a few of the buckets I thought might bail out my sinking ship:

• I will only drink at the weekends.
• I will only drink socially and never at home.
• I will drink a glass of water for every glass of alcohol I drink.
• I will take three months off the drink each year.
• I will only drink beer and no wine or spirits.
• I will only drink wine and with food as part of a meal.

Add to that list of ridiculous theories the expensive prescription drugs I turned to. The first I tried was Disulfiram, which interferes with the way your liver processes alcohol and makes you violently ill if you drink. The problem with this drug is that it relies on your discipline to take it every morning (alcoholics are not renowned for their discipline).

Initially, if I knew there was a big party or social occasion I was going to, I just wouldn't take it (and so begins the failure routine). Predictably I then loosened my rules further by only taking it Monday to Friday, allowing myself to drink at the weekends, I convinced myself that I deserved a treat at the weekends for being so good during the week.

The next stage of my defiance came when I resented the drug preventing me from drinking during the week and I experimented with it and found that I could just about tolerate a small beer while taking it. Any more than that and the side effects would knock me flat on my back. One night I pushed it a little further and had a large beer and a glass of wine. Within twenty minutes my head was pounding, my face blushing bright red, while my heart felt like it was trying to beat its way out of my chest cavity. For a moment I honestly thought I might die, and the only solution was to lie in a dark room motionless for several hours until the effects subsided.

I tried other drugs, such as Acamprosate Calcium, which interfere with the release of dopamine, essentially taking all the pleasure out of drinking. Over time it renders your favorite tipple as pleasurable as a soft drink, and logically you only want to drink one of those when you are thirsty. Again, with this drug the will-power or discipline required to take a daily tablet that ruins the very thing you are addicted to is a significant challenge. Add to that some pretty horrendous side effects from dizzy spells, insomnia, dry mouth and worse, and you start to think that feeling this bad to stay off the drink is simply not worth it.

Whether it's crazy routines or pills, they are all simply evidence of the ego's delusion that it is in some way in control. All these methods use some form of will-power that can't possibly work, because underneath the smoke screen you still believe that alcohol is a benefit that you are being deprived of.

Remember, there is no such thing as failure, things that go wrong are just events in the past, a time period we are no longer concerned with. If you finish reading this book and go three weeks without a drink and then slip up, the natural temptation (and the ego's opinion) is to think that this book doesn't work, you are not strong enough, or you are destined to always be a problem drinker. Recognize this belief for what it is; the conscious mind trying to predict the future – a skill it simply doesn't have. If you fall off the wagon… big deal, dust yourself down and carry on. When you wake in the morning, what is the point of beating yourself up about that mistake you made the night before? The past no longer exists.

Presumably you haven't woken up with a bottle in your hand having been drinking in your sleep somehow, so right there in that moment (where all of life is lived), you are not a drinker. Equally, now that we know that the future also doesn't exist and will never exist, the fact that you had a drink the night before has no bearing on whether you will have one later that day, tomorrow, the next day or ever again. Take each moment as it comes, every second that you decide you don't want to drink is a success.

The secret to stopping drinking is the same as the secret to get anything else in life that you want, and this is to remain in the moment. Don't make predictions about what sort of person you will be in the future. I wouldn't ask you to predict what will happen tomorrow anymore than I would ask you to perform open heart surgery on me, you simply don't have the skills to help me (of course, I am recklessly playing the numbers here, one day this book will land with an eminent heart surgeon and he will be mortally offended by that statement).

Your journey out of the mousetrap happens by being aware of our egoic mind; every time you find your mind wandering into the future or past, observe this happening from the point of view of an outsider. Disconnect yourself from the process; catch your ego at work.

For your conscious mind to have any power at all, it needs you to believe that you and it are one and the same thing. If you see if for what it really is; a minor part of your mind at work then it loses all its influence over you. Every time you catch your mind starting to worry, predict or reflect on past events and deliberately pull yourself back into the present moment you reduce its power over you by a fraction of one percent.

For most people the conscious mind seizes control of them tens of thousands of times a day, and so this process isn't a magic bullet cure. I can't promise if you do this ten times, twenty times or fifty times you will be cured, but then you didn't become alcohol dependent overnight, and no system out there can hope to restore the correct balance in a similar brief time period. Most other detox systems require a period of withdrawal, often called going 'cold turkey', which for an alcoholic is at best torturous, and in worst case scenarios can be fatal.

My method starts with your deep-seated desire to end this painful cycle and slowly deconstructs the obstacles preventing you from achieving your goal. Slowly, over time, as you keep resisting the attempted hijackings by your egoic mind you will feel a sense of peace begin to build. Once you get beyond the physical dependence on alcohol, your urge to drink is generated by the wants and needs of the ego, as this reduces so does your desire for alcohol.

A popular question at this point is "how long will it take?" I can't predict the future any more than you can, so won't even try to give you a specific prediction. For most people, once they understand that everything they previously believed about alcohol being a benefit was a big fat lie and can see that a chemical imbalance is causing pain for their ego to respond to, they simply stop. For a great many people that is directly after reading this book, others need a few weeks for the information to sink in, and others read the book several times before the penny drops.

Does alcohol affect your appearance?

"Sometimes we motivate ourselves by thinking of what we want to become. Sometimes we motivate ourselves by thinking about who we don't ever want to be again." – Shane Niemeyer

Another illusion of the Evil Clown is the transference of beauty. How many people wake up on a Sunday morning lying next to a dog ugly stranger, wondering where the stunning goddess or Greek Adonis they met the night before went to? I am sure nothing so unsavory has ever happened to you but rest assured, beer has been helping ugly people to have sex for hundreds of years – God bless it!

By now I hope you can see why I compare alcohol to some twisted evil clown. This substance, that we adamantly insist is nothing more than a social pleasantry can make us believe things have vanished before our eyes, it can steal our money without detection, make us see things that are not there at all and even makes us believe someone who looks like Kathy Bates is a gorgeous cat walk model who must be seduced at all costs!

Alcohol may make people appear to be significantly more attractive than they really are but while it is busy making silk purses out of sows' ears, the drug is actually taking payment for this trick directly from you. Drink alcohol heavily and you might as well play rugby because the ugly stick is coming to give you a good whacking either way!

Alcohol's effect on your skin is similar to its effect on the rest of your body: it steals the good hydration and leaves the bad (dryness, bloating and redness).

When you drink alcohol, it hinders the production of vasopressin, an anti-diuretic hormone. This causes your kidneys to work extra hard to remove excess water from your system, sending water to your bladder (and you to the restroom!) instead of your organs. Don't forget that your skin is the largest organ in the body, and drinking a lot of alcohol leaves it dehydrated.

When skin is dry, it is much more likely to wrinkle and make you look older than you are. Alcohol also robs your body of Vitamin A, which is essential for cell renewal and turnover, so your skin could take on a dull gray appearance. Staying hydrated will obviously have opposing effects: smoothing out wrinkles, leaving your skin looking bright, young and fresh. Drinking water is the only way to combat the drying effects of alcohol, hydrating from within.

Being so depleted of vital nutrients, electrolytes and fluids, your skin often shows signs of bloating and swelling. When you're lacking what you need, your body will store whatever it can get, wherever it can, and any water you take in will cause your tissues to swell.

Alcohol can also affect pre-existing conditions like rosacea, causing it to worsen or flare up more often.

Alcohol increases your blood flow, often causing blood vessels in your face to dilate (sometimes permanently) and often burst, leaving behind broken capillaries and red spots that are difficult to get rid of.

When you drink alcohol, it's broken down into acetate (basically vinegar), which the body will burn before any other calorie you've consumed or stored, including fat or even sugar. So if you drink and consume more calories than you need, you're more likely to store the fat from the Twinkie ™ you ate and the sugar from the Coke ™ you drank because your body is getting all its energy from the acetate in the beer you sucked down. Further, studies show that alcohol temporarily inhibits "lipid oxidation" in other words, when alcohol is in your system, it's harder for your body to burn fat that's already there.

Your body has a set number of calories needed to maintain your weight. This need is based on your height, weight, age, gender, and activity level. When you consume more calories than your body needs, you will gain weight. Alcohol can lead to weight gain from the calories it provides and by causing you to eat more calories after consuming the alcohol.

It's easy to forget that you can drink as many calories as you eat. In fact, some drinks can have as many calories as a meal! The next time you reach for a cocktail before your meal consider if it's worth the weight that you could be gaining from it.

Research has shown a 20% increase in calories consumed at a meal when alcohol was consumed before the meal. There was a total caloric increase of 33% when the calories from the alcohol were added. Along with the increase in weight you can have an increased risk to your health because of where you gain the weight.

A study of over 3,000 people showed that consuming elevated amounts of alcohol is associated with abdominal obesity in men.

Many people joke about this being a "beer belly." Unfortunately, a "beer belly" puts you at an increased risk for type 2 diabetes, elevated blood lipids, hypertension, and cardiovascular disease.

The late-night munchies are often associated with a night of drinking. Have you ever realized that anytime you drink alcohol you are hungrier or you end up eating more than usual?

Studies have shown that in the short term, alcohol stimulates food intake and can also increase feelings of hunger. Having your judgment impaired and stimulating your appetite is a recipe for failure if you are trying to follow a weight-loss plan.

In short if you drink heavily you are going to have to accept something I call the two tens. The fact that you are going to generally look ten years older than you really are and you are going to die at least ten years before your time. Of course every coin has a flip side and removing alcohol permanently will show you the other side of the coin.

But I genuinely like the taste of alcohol!

"Character cannot be developed in ease and quiet. Only through experience of trial and suffering can the soul be strengthened, ambition inspired, and success achieved." – Helen Keller

Most people who drink wine every day claim they honestly like the taste of it. This is nonsense; alcohol tastes so bad that the drinks manufacturers mostly have to find increasingly potent ways to cover it up. The body is an amazing and sophisticated piece of natural engineering.

Despite what lies you have taught yourself on a superficial level, you still cannot break the rules your body has created over millions of years of evolution. Right at the top of our hierarchy of needs is the need to protect life, to stay alive at all costs. This is hardwired into every cell, every molecule and every tiny atom of your being. You can't decide to stop your heart beating or never to breathe again. You can't because it breaks the ultimate built-in rule; that of ensuring self-preservation at all costs.

The reason pure alcohol tastes terrible is the same reason rotting meat or moldy, fungus infested bread tastes terrible. Your body is warning you that you are consuming something that is putting you at risk. Think about it, in a hospital operating theatre, the room and the entire medical team that works in it must be 100% free of germs, bacteria, and viral contaminants. So what do they scrub their hands with; not soap but alcohol. Because instantly, on contact with any living organisms, it kills them dead! It pulls every bit of moisture out of their cells and causes them to implode in on themselves. At a microcellular level, alcohol is akin to thermonuclear war; nothing survives.

Do you honestly believe you have some fantastic internal system to get around this fact? Somehow, when you consume this dangerous disinfectant, it 'doesn't do the same level of damage because you have hidden it in a bit of cranberry juice.

Alcohol tastes horrible, you already know this but have forgotten, or as is more accurate, you have conditioned yourself to believe the opposite. As a hypnotherapist, I can tell you that this is entirely possible and can be easily replicated in a relatively short space of time to prove the point. In hypnosis, the conscious (thinking and judging) mind is bypassed, which means I can speak directly to the subconscious and implant beliefs without interference from the ego. Obviously, in therapy (and what you will find on the hypnosis tracks that accompany this book – available in the member's area) all suggestions are positive and delivered for your benefit, but it is entirely possible for me to condition you to enjoy something deeply unpleasant, such as a hard punch on the arm! If while under hypnosis, I hit you hard but told you it felt amazing and repeated that process many times and over several sessions, you would eventually begin to crave the experience.

You can see this feature of the human mind demonstrated in the most horrendous situations. When people are held captive by a sole individual and despite the fact that this person has abducted them, tortured and abused them, the victim slowly over time begins to develop feelings for the perpetrator.

Despite suffering at the hands of this person, they become conditioned to their environment and begin to want to please the person who holds them against their will. This phenomenon has been studied at length by eminent psychologists and is known as "Stockholm syndrome".

To a certain degree, I believe you are suffering from a form of this syndrome; alcohol has abused you for so long that you now firmly believe there is a benefit to you. You have fallen in love with a killer!

I say again, alcohol tastes bad; your first interaction with it proved that point. When you first sneaked a drink of your 'father's neat whiskey, did it taste amazing? Or did it taste vile? Most people will say it tasted disgusting and they 'couldn't ever imagine getting hooked on something that tasted that bad. The taste of alcohol has not changed, so the only explanation for your current belief that it tastes good, is that you have changed. You have conditioned yourself to believe alcohol tastes good. 'Don't feel bad; you have had a significant helping hand from society and the advertising industry.

What you must understand from this point on is that what you previously believed about booze was a lie and nothing more. If I poured a glass of pure alcohol and asked you to dip your little finger in and taste it, I am sure you will agree it would taste horrible, indeed, if you drank that glass of liquid you would shortly be dead.

Funny really because since birth you have been programmed to ignore this and instead believe that alcohol is natural and an everyday part of life that you must consume if you are to be considered by your peers as a fun and social member of the gang. This is a throwback to our primitive evolution, we are still pack animals to a certain extent, and this is another reason for our global addiction to this drug.

The second reason is best explained by a smarter man than I, a famous psychologist called Abraham Maslow. Maslow is known for establishing the theory of a hierarchy of needs, writing that human beings are motivated by unsatisfied needs and that certain lower needs need to be satisfied before higher needs can be.

Although there is a continuous cycle of human wars, murder, and deceit, he believed that violence is not what human nature is meant to be like. Violence and other evils occur when human needs are thwarted. In other words, people who are deprived of lower needs, such as safety, may defend themselves by violent means. He did not believe that humans are violent because they enjoy violence. Or that they lie, cheat, and steal because they enjoy doing it.

According to Maslow, there are general types of needs (physiological, safety, love, and esteem), and they must be satisfied before a person can act unselfishly. He called these needs "deficiency needs". As long as we are motivated to satisfy these cravings, we are moving towards growth, toward self-actualization.

Satisfying needs is healthy, and blocking gratification makes us sick and unhappy. In other words, we are all "needs junkies" with cravings that must be satisfied and should be satisfied. If we don't concentrate on doing this, we will literally become sick.

"Will-power" is an illusionary weapon created by the egoic mind. 'It's like your enemy giving you a plastic sword and saying "here, use this to protect yourself if I ever attack you!" This is exactly why people have such a hard time trying to go cold turkey with their drinking. One morning you wake up and say, 'that's it I am never drinking again. By lunchtime, you have a psychological itch so intense you are almost screaming inside.

Will-power does not work because it forces your subconscious and conscious mind into civil war. The exact same reason why the moment you go on a diet, you become hungrier than you thought possible.

Here is the secret to stopping drinking; you need to attach more pleasure to not drinking than there is to drinking. You have to remove the need by understanding the truth about booze. It is not a social pleasantry but rather an attractively packaged poison. A multi-billion dollar marketing campaign for the alcoholic drinks industry is working exceptionally hard to convince you otherwise, but you have to trust your gut on this one.

Let me put the point another way. I have two wonderful children who I love and adore more than life itself. Maybe you also have children yourself, and you can understand my love and need to protect my children from the harms of the world? Let me ask you a question: If you had some strong rat poison for dealing with a tricky vermin infestation, would you keep it in a chocolate box and put it within reach of your kids?

Of course not! But alcohol is packaged exactly like that. Booze is sold in pretty elegant bottles. Surely something in such exquisite packaging must taste amazing right?

Alcohol is similar to an anti-personnel landmine. You step on it, and beyond a small clunk, all appears fine… until you try and step off it. Then and only then you discover what a mess you are really in.

Our desire to drink is what we call a proponent need; this is a "need" that has a powerful influence over our actions. Everyone has proponent needs, but those "needs" will vary among individuals. A teenager may have a need to feel that he/she is accepted by a group. A heroin addict will need to satisfy his/her cravings for heroin to function normally in society, and because of the strength of the need, they are unlikely to worry about acceptance by other people.

There is no difference between alcohol and heroin or alcohol and nicotine. The only difference is alcohol is socially acceptable. But ask yourself this, if it had not yet been invented and I brought it to market tomorrow, do you think I would get it even halfway through the rigorous testing process modern day food and beverages have to go through?

Around the world there is a very popular television program called 'Dragon's Den', where would-be entrepreneurs pitch their ideas to already successful venture capitalists seeking investment. Can you imagine taking your fabulous new drink additive called alcohol before the Dragons and asking them to invest?

Entrepreneur: "Hello Dragons… I am here to ask for $1,000,000,000 to launch my new drink supplement called alcohol. Would you like to try a glass?"

A small sample of the product is poured into shot glasses for each of the investors in turn; cautiously they take a sip…

Dragons: "My God that tastes disgusting!"

Entrepreneur: "Yes, it does initially, but we have tested it quite extensively and find that people do eventually become accustomed to the taste. Plus, we use sweet tasting carrier beverages such as orange juice and cola to cover up the real taste. When they get used to it the consumer will feel amazing! Parties will go with a bang, everything seems funnier, and there is a massive euphoric sense of well being".

Dragons: "Sounds interesting, are there any down sides to this new drink?"

Entrepreneur: "Erm, well there is a slight risk of vomiting, sexually transmitted disease from unprotected sex, not to mention the violence and serious damage to careers, reputations and relationships. You probably need to be aware that several millions of our potential customers will have to die in agony from organ failure. Apart from that, I think this product has great potential".

Dragons: "I am not investing in that, I am out!"

Don't take stop drinking advice off other drinkers!

"We may think there is willpower involved, but more likely … change is due to want power. Wanting the new addiction more than the old one. Wanting the new me in preference to the person I am now." –
George Sheehan

I have noticed a common theme among alcohol addicts. They tend to ask other drinkers for advice on how to stop drinking. It should seem obvious that this is a mistake, because these people don't have the first clue.

So why do we do this?

Firstly it's not something unique to drinkers. I write books on various self-help subjects from wealth creation to escaping the nine to five. I have noticed that people who want more money tend to ask people who don't have any for advice. People looking for an escape from the rat race ask their work colleagues for guidance.

In a way it's entirely understandable. When we are making big decisions in life. Such as setting up our own business, investing our savings or quitting drinking, we want the guidance and support that comes from people who have our back. We turn first to the people who love and care about us.

For most of the people who join my Stop Drinking Program their alcohol problem is mainly hidden from the outside world. They are entirely functioning people and most will not have the slightest clue just how much they are struggling with alcohol.

Back when I was a drinker I was the director of two major businesses and the patron of a regional children's charity. Everyone knew I could handle my drink and was always the first to the bar but nobody knew that I woke up every morning ripped apart by the guilt and regret of how much I drank the night before.

Often you don't want your drinking habit to become public knowledge because there is a strange and illogical stigma attached to it. Alcoholism can damage your reputation, invalidate your medical insurance and hinder your career. So perhaps it's entirely understandable that people turn to loved ones for advice.

The problem with this is two fold. Your alcohol drinking friend or family member hasn't got the first clue how to stop drinking. However, because they love you and care about you, they won't just want to turn you away without offering some help.

The second problem is the advice they offer often doesn't help and may even give you false hope. Drinkers may listen to how much you are drinking and tell you not to worry because you are drinking less than them.

When I first mentioned my drinking to a doctor he told me not to panic because I wasn't so far ahead of what he was drinking. This did actually reassure me that I was fine to carry on. Hey, I had a great excuse – a qualified doctor told me not to worry.

The doctor probably only said that because to tell me that what I was doing what dangerous would be to also confront his own addiction.

This is a 'difficult to spot' deception. The person you are asking for advice may very well be also struggling with their drinking. Functioning alcoholics are everywhere and often completely indistinguishable from sober folk. So let's take a look at some common, well-intentioned statements and dissect them to understand where they are coming from:

I drink more than you! You must think I am such a mess.

This is a very subtle one that pulls on your good intentions towards your friend or family member. Here they appear to be trying to reassure you about the amount you are drinking. However there is an underlying command of 'if you love me have a drink, so I don't feel like you are judging me'.

Nonsense I will get you a drink.

Here they are taking a dominant position over you, very much like a parent would do. They appear to be absolving you of blame but in reality you drinking has nothing to do with what you get out of the activity. Your fellow drinker knows that he/she has a problem and demands you provide the social proof they need to carry on.

You're different when you don't drink, more sensible.

Calling someone sensible should be a compliment but in this case you understand only too well what is really being said. The drinker is suggesting that they don't like being around you when you don't drink.

Come on, just have one. What's the worst that can happen?

Problem drinkers know only too well that there is no such thing as 'just one drink'. They have repeatedly failed to apply that rule to themselves so they are aware that you won't be able to either.

It's true that it's unlikely anything bad will happen if you choose to drink alcohol in that moment. You won't drop down dead, spontaneously combust or develop cancer in that precise moment. The question 'what's the worst that can happen' is a loaded dice. It forces you to answer the question out of context.

By all means get the support of those that love you but if they are also trapped in the alcoholism loop don't seek their guidance. Get your information from people who have been there and escaped. Read the highly rated books on Amazon by other recovering alcoholics, watch videos on YouTube and read the blogs of people who know how you feel.

When it comes to alcohol – you should trust me on this – it is the truth that will set you free!

"Let me tell you something you already know. The world ain't all sunshine and rainbows. It is a very mean and nasty place and it will beat you to your knees and keep you there permanently if you let it. You, me, or nobody is gonna hit as hard as life. But it ain't how hard you hit; it's about how hard you can get hit, and keep moving forward. How much you can take, and keep moving forward. That's how winning is done. Now, if you know what you're worth, then go out and get what you're worth. But you gotta be willing to take the hit, and not pointing fingers saying you ain't where you are because of him, or her, or anybody. Cowards do that and that ain't you. You're better than that", Rocky Balboa

Sandra T. emailed me this morning and asked how you deal with relapse. She says she was doing great and loving the program and then 4 days in she had one drink and it led to several more.

Actually what Sandra is describing there I would not consider to be 'relapsing'. The way my stop drinking program works is by flipping a switch in your head. It is an entirely binary process, it's not a dial, it is a two-way switch. You are either a drinker or not, you either want to drink or you don't. There is no middle ground and there is no drinking in moderation.

If you have been sober for six months to a year or longer and you have a drink I would consider this to be a true relapse. But the reasons for this are entirely different to why people return to drink in the early stages. We will come back to that type of relapse in a moment. There are two more types of 'falling off the wagon' that apply more to the early stages of sobriety.

The First Two to Three Weeks

If you drink alcohol within the first couple of weeks of quitting you were simply beaten by the 'kick' from the drug. All addictive substances have a mechanism to apply pressure on you to try and make you 'use' again.

Alcohol makes you feel uncomfortable and disguises the sensation as mild anxiety or the same way you feel when you are a little stressed out. If you respond to the 'kick' by drinking it rewards you by removing the discomfort it created in the first place – mission accomplished.

During the first couple of weeks you just have to understand what is going on and tough it out. During this time your new hobby needs to become 'understanding the truth about alcohol'. Fill your head with good information constantly. Seriously, you need to get obsessed about what you are doing. Become an alcohol bore!

The First Six Months

If you drink alcohol once you are outside the 'kick' then this is simply an indicator that you still believe that there is a benefit to drinking. If you didn't believe there were any benefits you just wouldn't drink.

Most drinkers don't also use heroin. But why? It feels much better than alcohol so why not use it?

Even people who claim to have an 'addictive personality' don't use heroin! However, not many people believe that adding heroin to their lives would be an enhancement. Most right thinking individuals would believe the opposite to be true. Heroin would be entirely destructive and harmful to their lives.

Because this is their firmly held belief, they never feel tempted to shoot up!

If you feel tempted to drink it is because you believe doing so would provide a benefit or solve a problem. Whether that is to help you relax, help you sleep or simply to stop your overactive mind.

The truth is all those beliefs are erroneous. All those supposed benefits are an illusion created by the drug. There is not one single benefit to alcohol – not a single one! You need to address this slip by going back into learning mode and re-starting the journey. Listen to the hypnosis tracks, read the books, watch the videos. Become OCD about getting the truth from your conscious mind into your subconscious belief structure.

Six Months Onwards

If you have been sober for more than six months then you are into the true area of potential relapse. Normally after one year the former drinker has lost clarity on just how painfully addicted to alcohol they were.

They start to get a little cocky in their thinking. Escaping alcohol now seems to have been so easy. For a whole year they have lived an amazing life free of the drug and they didn't find it difficult. They start to wonder if they have been 'cured' and now they can control alcohol.

When you start thinking like this you should sound the warning sirens and wave red flags all over the place. This is a very dangerous place to be. Because the next thing you start thinking is 'perhaps I can just have one drink'.

"Just one drink" are the three most lethal words you will ever say or think. The hard reality is, we spent decades physically altering our brain so that it lights up like a Christmas tree whenever we drink alcohol. We can never go back to normal drinking – ever!

'Just one drink' will lead to a self-destructive relapse that could take months or years to escape from. You will go back and use the same process to stop drinking as you did before. But now it's ten times harder because your faith in the system has been damaged by the relapse. Instead of being 100% confident in the program, now you are only 70% confident and this makes you panic that there is really no escape from the drug.

All relapse is avoidable if you are fully aware of what is coming, and you understand what to expect.

For example, imagine you had a bad car accident one Tuesday afternoon on the highway. A car crossed into the wrong lane and totaled your car.

Now imagine if a magic genie had visited you a week prior to the accident and said 'Be careful driving on Tuesday – something bad will happen on the highway'. Of course you can still have the accident but with the forewarning you have a much better chance of avoiding it. That is exactly what this is… your forewarning.

I drink because life is too short!

"When you get into a tight place and everything goes against you, till it seems you could not hang on a minute longer, never give up then, for that is just the place and time that the tide will turn." – Harriet Beecher Stowe

I drink because life's too short… Or perhaps life is too short because you drink?

Many people defend their use of alcohol with statements that on first hearing sound entirely laudable. Statements such as 'I drink, so what? I am not hurting anyone else', 'I drink because life is too short' and I have even heard 'so us drinkers live a shorter life, but we live a better life'. Would you believe a pharmacist friend of mine said that last one!

All these assumptions are based on a lie or as we call it these days 'an alternative truth'. The assumption that alcohol is a benefit with some side effects. The reality is, alcohol is a problem with life limiting side effects.

I drink, so what? I am not hurting anyone else:

It's my life, keep out of my business! This is a common defense offered by problem drinkers everywhere. While concerned family members express concern about their drinking and try encourage them to get help.

The problem is this is not true. You see, your own death is not really going to hurt you personally. It is only the death of other people that you will be forced to suffer.

You are free to carry on drinking, but don't be under any illusion that you are only hurting yourself. Trust me on this, when you start getting ill and still refuse to stop drinking your friends and family will have plenty of sleepless nights as they witness your self-destruction.

When you get the fatal diagnosis that you have something terminal, it will be your family that will torture themselves that they didn't try hard enough to get you help. It will be your children and your partner who have to consider life without you.

When you die, it will be your loved ones who cry at your grave and feel your loss. Drinkers need to wake up to the fact that their drinking is not just 'their business'.

I drink because life is too short!

No, you drink because you are addicted to a drug. Anyone who makes a statement such as this is blissfully unaware of how alcohol works.

Alcohol is the most devious and insidious drug on planet earth. Just because it is licensed and endorsed by the government does not make it safe. I don't know about the political system where you live but personally I wouldn't just my countries politicians to find there asshole with both hands.

Alcohol creates pain and misery purely to motivate the addict to drink. When they drink alcohol the drug rewards the individual by removing the discomfort it placed there in the first place.

Back when I was a drinker, I wanted to quit but I was in a panic about whether life would be worth living without alcohol… I was worried I would have no way to relax etc. It took me a while to realize that the drug was creating all the things I was using alcohol to escape from. Remove the source and you no longer need the solution!

Us drinkers live a shorter life, but we live a better life!

This is on a similar misguided theme as the 'I drink because life is too short'. I don't need to explain the broken logic any further.

However, what I do want to mention, is the person who first used this expression with me. I have a friend who is perhaps the wisest, most present individual I know. He runs a chain of Pharmacies in Cyprus, as you can imagine – a very intelligent and informed individual.

As smart as he is, he still opens half a bottle of whiskey every other day. When I first questioned his drinking, he shrugged in that cool Greek way, lit a cigarette and said 'So we live a shorter life, but we live a better life my friend'.

I think what he is referring to there is a statistic that heavy drinkers live on average ten years less than a non drinker or moderate drinker. However, to assume that you just live an amazing life and just die in your sleep one night, ten years early is to miss the likely way life will end for a drinker.

Alcohol is a proven carcinogenic, for example - women who drink have a 50% increased chance of developing breast cancer. Men have a vastly increased risk of prostate cancer and so on. Since the 1990's it has no longer been a case that alcohol might cause cancer. We now know for certain that alcohol DOES cause cancer.

So perhaps instead of dropping down dead one day in a blaze of glory, you develop cancer. You have years for painful chemotherapy and eventually waste away to nothing. Or maybe your liver fails and you spend six month in agony hoping against all the odds to get a liver transplant. Eventually there is so much poison in your body you collapse a die.

Seriously wake up and grow up!

Alcohol kills someone every 90 seconds, it is the second most addictive substance behind heroin. It is the ultimate wolf in sheep's clothes.

Alcohol has one objective, to kill you. It will do everything to distract your attention while it is busy achieving this goal. The first step on your happy sober journey is to stop denying the reality.

Face the truth, embrace the truth and then set about changing the way you think, talk and feel about alcohol. This is the process I used to break a near two decade long relationship with a killer!

"The Evil Clown is always on the other side of the door, waiting. The secret is to never open it", Craig Beck

A few weeks ago I recorded a video blog about the illusion that alcohol tastes good. Someone on YouTube took issue with the post and suggested that I was wrong because 'nothing tastes better than a cold beer in the sunshine'.

His comment reminded me of something that happened to me a few years ago. On the day in question a heat wave was hitting the town and temperatures were over 40 degrees. My friend and I had been scuba diving and decided to stop off at a bar on the way home to quench our thirst.

I ordered a diet Coke and he ordered a beer. I noticed that there was a huge difference in the way the two drinks were served. My drink came first. A diet coke in a straight glass was placed in front of me and the barman held his hand out for three euros.

However, the serving of my friends beer was a much more theatrical experience. A frozen glass was taken out of the freezer; it made a magical crackling sound as the cold glass hit the warm arm. Instantly condensation started to run sensually down the frosted glass.

But it wasn't just any sort of glass... this thing was a chalice. An intricately carved trophy that Zeus himself would be proud to drink from.

Next a branded beer mat was placed in front of my friend while beer was poured from a beautiful silver beer tap, a giant silver swan neck spouting a golden amber liquid.

This beautiful piece of art was placed in front of my friend and the barman held his hand out for the €1.60. Seriously, is it any wonder that the illusion of beer being great in the sunshine has gained so much traction?

Why does us sober individuals get treated so badly by bars & pubs?

The alcohol manufacturers know full well that a non-drinker is going to have one or two drinks, maximum! However, they also know that even if a drinker only intends to have one drink, the drug will blow all their good intentions out of the water within minutes of the first sip.

I can understand it from both sides of the bar. Quite often when I am with friends in a pub I will have a couple of glasses of tonic water. By the time it gets to the third round of drinks and I am asked what I want. The answer I normally give is 'nothing I am not thirsty'. Non-drinkers only really drink to appease their thirst and then they stop.

Drinkers however are not downing pint after pint of liquid because they are thirsty. This is perhaps why teetotalers are treated with such passive aggressive contempt by bars, pubs and restaurants around the world.

The other thing about soft drinks and water is it's hard to upsell a customer to a better brand. Drinkers will occasionally treat themselves to an expensive bottle of wine or buy a $100 bottle of champagne to impress their dinner guests. You would struggle to impress anyone by asking the waiter to bring you the finest bottle of Coca-Cola they have.

Most restaurants don't make a profit on the food they serve. It is the over priced booze served by the snooty wine Semillon that generates the profit. So imagine how the restaurant owner feels when he realizes he has a table full of non-drinkers! They know that drinkers won't just have one drink. Plus when you also play on the laziness of drinkers you have a table full of ATM's.

I learnt a very expensive lesson on board a cruise ship once. My friend Geoff and I were working at a radio station in the North West of England. The station had arranged a listener trip aboard the famous Queen Elizabeth II cruise liner. Geoff and I were encouraged to get as many listeners as possible signed up. We were informed that if we sold 50 places on the ship we could both go for free.

We ended up selling 70 tickets and were very happy to have a drunken week away on board the most luxurious cruise ship in the world.

It was the most pampered and looked after I have ever felt. You don't need cash on board; you only need to vaguely look like you want something and a waiter is by your side within seconds. Any drink you want is never more than thirty seconds away. Even money is delivered when you want it! If you want a couple of hundred dollars in casino chips to play roulette, just put your hand in the air and they will be in your possession before you can say 'just sign here sir'.

Honestly, I felt like James Bond. I was wearing a tux and drinking gallons of the very best Martini (shaken not stirred). However, just like alcohol this whole 007 lifestyle was just an illusion. At the end of the vacation as the ship was returning to dock in Southampton. I had to stagger, with a crazy bad hangover to the purser's office to pay my bill.

I reached for the credit card in pure shame as I was presented with a bar and casino bill of over $3000. At the time that was a significant amount of money and certainly something that I was going to have to keep secret from my wife. The cruise liner had treated me like a king and then billed me like a king. All because they know that drinkers will keep drinking, especially if you make it super easy for them.

Alcohol is such a devious drug that the very first thing it does is interfere with the part of the brain responsible for making sound decisions. This is why us 'problem drinkers' have such a hard time just having one drink.

Think about that for a moment, it is very much how wars are fought. When two armies attack each other, one of the first objectives is to disable the defenses of the opposing army.

"If you know the enemy and know yourself, you need not fear the result of a hundred battles. If you know yourself but not the enemy, for every victory gained you will also suffer a defeat. If you know neither the enemy nor yourself, you will succumb in every battle",
Sun Tzu, The Art of War

To beat alcohol and get it out of your life, you have to know your enemy. Alcohol is not playing fair; it's attacking you and at the same time pretending to be your friend. While you are busy watching the theatre and drama that I described above, this insidious drug is working towards its only goal.

Alcohol is not your friend; it is your worst enemy. It has only one goal – to kill you and it will not stop until it achieves that outcome.

Dating after quitting drinking – how is that supposed to work?

"The one thing I know for sure is that feelings are rarely mutual, so when they are, drop everything, forget belongings and expectations, forget the games, the two days between texts, the hard to gets because this is it, this is what the entire world is after and you've stumbled upon it by chance, by accident—so take a deep breath, take a step forward, now run, collide like planets in the system of a dying sun, embrace each other with both arms and let all the rules, the opinions and common sense crash down around you. Because this is love kid, and it's all yours. Believe me, you're in for one hell of a ride, after all—this is the one thing I know for sure." — Beau Taplin

Alcohol causes serious damage to relationships, that much is obvious. However, it also covers up problems and dysfunction in your relationship. When you quit drinking you are faced with a choice, to repair the damage alcohol has done to your relationship or to address the issues that alcohol was making you avoid dealing with.

When I stopped drinking my marriage also came to an end. I am not saying that quitting drinking caused the collapse of my marriage. Rather it was a period in my life where I decided I needed to learn how to love myself. I dumped this poison out of my life; I lost some weight and started taking better care of myself. I also decided that I wasn't happy and needed to make some dramatic changes in my life.

The short story is, I ended up being sober and single for the first time in nearly two decades. Whether you are in a similar experienced position or young free and single it is natural to worry about how you date and avoid alcohol at the same time.

The good news is, while appears that alcohol and dating are intrinsically linked. Dating without booze is actually much better and much more rewarding.

You may worry that you will be more nervous and less confident without a little glass of Dutch Courage but as I have previously explained: Alcohol doesn't make you confident it just makes you stupid. You are less risk adverse and likely to charge ahead not because you are braver but rather because your intellectual capacity has been compromised.

I also remember going on drunken dates. I would start the evening not being very attracted to the woman I was talking to. However, the more I drunk the more attractive she became to me. Again that might sound like a benefit but imagine what happens the next morning when the booze has worn off.

On the flip side, ask yourself 'do you really think women are impressed by the drunken, slurring approaches of men who need alcohol before they can act'?

What I discovered, to my shock, was that some women refuse to date you when they find out that you don't drink alcohol. When you get rejected for this reason it is easy to feel resentment toward your sobriety. This is a mistake, because you have actually been saved from wasting you time dating an alcoholic.

Only fellow 'problem drinkers' will refuse to date a teetotaler. They know it would cause them huge psychological pain to be with this person. They would have to sneak drinks when the other person wasn't looking to try and portray their drinking as 'normal'.

If you want to make your life 1000% better then your goal should be to be in a relationship with someone who drinks in moderation or, even better, not at all!

I was in a long-term relationship with a woman who had a drink problem and it broke my heart. While I was never tempted to join her, it hurt to see a bright and intelligent woman turn into a stupid, brainless zombie.

Today I am in a beautiful relationship. My partner Daniela drinks about 2 beers a year! That means we never have alcohol in the house, neither of us ever waste a weekend in bed suffering with a hangover and we never upset each other with silly drunken mistakes.

Women Prefer Sober Guys

Forgive me if this answer is geared toward men, it's just written from my own personal experience.

Women who are looking for a long-term relationship have certain filters. They want a man of value who is a successful, reliable provider. I do not mean they are looking for a man to pay for their every whim. Just that he is mature and responsible enough to hold down a decent job and make her proud of him.

There are a couple of things that you can bring up on a first date that will set huge alarm bells ringing in the mind of many women. It should go without saying that a relaxed view on infidelity is a big no-no. However, mention that you love to go to the casino or start every anecdote with "one time when I was drunk' and she will have red flags all over the place.

Many women have experienced the pain of being in a relationship with an addict. They know that whether it's booze or gambling, it will ultimately lead to a dishonest and painful relationship.

Sober guys are more valuable!

Aesthetically there are many benefits to dating without alcohol too. The hard reality is, non-drinkers just look better. They take better care of themselves and invest more in their appearance. Drinkers spend most of their spare cash on booze. They look tired, blotchy, bloated and tend to be overweight.

Stop worrying about taking the alcohol out of dating. When you understand the truth behind the smokescreen you will realize it's a huge benefit for everyone involved.

How do you get the mindset to quit drinking and stay quit?

"The hardest struggle of all is to be something different from what the average man is. I don't believe in 'super-men,' for the world is full of capable men, but it's the fellow with determination that wins out", Charles M. Schwab

At the back of my house there is a huge multi gym. It cost me a lot of money and I hate it! I hate it with a passion, everyday when I walk past it I swear profusely at it.

However, everyday without fail, I spend forty minutes using it. I don't do it because I enjoy it or because I want to look like a muscle man. I use it because I understand the consequences of not using it and I recognize the benefits of putting the effort in.

I am nearly 43 years old and I understand that the aches and pains I feel these days are only going to get worse if I don't take action. Nobody is going to fix this problem for me and excuses are going to get me nothing but permission to fail.

Quitting drinking requires the same determination, maturity and focus. You can't half-heartedly stop drinking, you are either committed to this decision or you are not.

I see a recurring theme in the Stop Drinking Expert Facebook group. Somebody will confess to a moment of weakness the night before and reveal that they fell off the wagon. This will be followed by a series of well meaning and supportive comments expressing empathy and sympathy.

This is not helpful!

Doing this would be the same as me coming up with a daily excuse to not use the multi-gym and then looking for sympathy from Daniela when she comes home from work.

"Oh Daniela, it's so terrible. I wanted to use the multi gym but then I felt a bit sick and decided to sit in front of the TV instead… how awful it's been for me"

Everyday I think of an excuse not to exercise and every day I have a choice as to whether I use the excuse or I act like a grown up and do what is required of me.

Once you are outside the physical kick of the drug, which last a few weeks and no more. You are into the territory of psychological issues and anchors. This is no different to other choices that you make on a daily basis.

When you choose to drink (because lets be honest, it is your decision – nobody pours it into your mouth) you are choosing to be a victim. Taking the path of least resistance nearly always gets you a poor outcome.

Think about it… it would be easier to sit at home than to get up every morning and go to work. It would be easier for me to throw a sheet over the multi-gym and forget I ever bought the bloody thing and it would be easier to just pour the glass of wine and drink it.

But, would any of those choices benefit you in the long run?

Of course not! So this is where you have to take responsibility for making the right choice. You are entirely capable of doing this because you prove it in other areas on a daily basis.

I am not writing this to bully you or patronize you. Actually, I want to encourage you to get motivated about this part of your life. I firmly believe that if you want to quit, and more importantly 'stay quit' then you have to adopt a binary mindset about this.

Quitting drinking is easy; just don't put alcohol in your mouth... there you've done it. Staying quit is about the choices you make on an ongoing basis.

It's easier to make good decisions when you have good data to base them upon.

For example: If your child asked if they could go on a school trip abroad, you wouldn't just say yes without first asking some important questions and doing a little research. Perhaps after speaking to the school and some other parents, if you were comfortable that it was safe and sensible you may decide to allow your child the trip.

Quitting drinking is an important decision in your life. So, make sure you have a head full of good and correct information to allow you to make wise choices. When you get the temptation to have 'just one glass of wine' if you know for 100% certainty that the drug is going to disable your ability to make rational decisions and deliberately try to force you to drink more, then it is easy to make a choice that will serve you in a positive way.

I use the multi gym everyday because I understand that only I can make the choices required to ensure I am fit, healthy and happy. Quitting drinking is the same; actually it is the ultimate act of self-respect.

Of course quitting an addictive drug is not easy. If it were easy then I would not be writing this book. You will notice that there is no such website as stopeatingpeanutsexpert.com. You know why? Because if you start eating too many peanuts, you just stop doing it – job done.

If you are serious about beating this problem then you have to fight, and fight hard. Nobody is motivated to go the gym because they love the equipment or because they really enjoy getting changed back and forth into sweat pants. People go to a gym because they fall in love with the end result of their effort, dedication and determination.

Legendary boxer Mohammed Ali famously revealed that he hated every single second of training. However, he made a committed decision to ignore the short-term discomfort, in order to live the rest of his life as a champion. I encourage you to get the same eye of the tiger mentality. You must decide now to take on the Evil Clown and give him the fight of his life.

Float like a butterfly and sting like a bee.

Take ownership of this challenge, become obsessive about learning the truth about this drug and use the weight of this knowledge to help you make empowering decisions.

"I believe that the greatest gift you can give your family and the world is a healthy you", Joyce Meyer

Alcohol is processed predominantly by the liver and while this amazing organ can take a monumental amount of abuse and keep functioning, it has its limitations.

You have to marvel at the power and resilience of the human liver. It can take decades of continuous poison and still keep doing what it does. It even has the ability to self-repair and regenerate. Actually medical scientists can now grow a complete full size liver from a tiny piece of a healthy donor organ.

However, it is not made of steel and if you keep drinking poison for fun, there will come a point where it can no longer keep going. But think about it; imagine if you dipped your right hand in bleach three times a day for thirty years – how do you think your hand would look when compared to the left hand?

Can you reverse liver damage? Yes, but it depends on the type of damage.

If you have a dull ache in your right flank then you should sit up and take notice. Don't spend a year trying to prove it's nothing to do with your alcohol consumption – like I did!

The right side pain commonly reported by problem drinkers is the first sign that your liver is in trauma. You may assume that if it was a serious problem then it would generate serious pain – but this is just yet another trapdoor for the alcoholic.

The liver organ does not have any nerve endings. So it can be considerably damaged and you won't know the first thing about it. This is why so many drinkers find out too late that they have fatal cirrhosis.

Of course you may take solace in the hope that a liver transplant is an option. However, the average wait for a suitable liver donor is over one year. A diagnosis of end stage cirrhosis is going to give you six months to live at the most.

There is no dialysis machine for the liver as there is for the kidneys. For most alcoholics with liver damage they are killed first by the alcohol and second by the supply and demand problem of transplantation.

The liver is like a big sponge, when it is healthy. It should be soft and flexible but alcohol causes serious damage to the cells. Eventually scar tissue starts to form where these repeated injuries occur. Scar tissue is hard, inflexible and entirely useless to you. If you keep drinking and allow this scar tissue to keep expanding you eventually get to the point where you don't have enough functioning liver left to filter the toxins from your blood.

Scar tissue once formed cannot be reversed. However, if you stop drinking you can prevent the situation getting fatally worse.

The other common problem reported by drinkers is a fatty liver. This is what I was suffering from and if I had not stopped drinking I would have slowly moved into the dangerous complication of liver cirrhosis.

Fatty liver happens when unwanted fat accumulates inside liver cells. This means healthy, well-balanced liver organ tissue becomes partly replaced with fatty tissue. The fat starts to attack the liver, gradually infiltrating the healthy liver regions, so that less and less strong liver cells remains. The fatty liver has a yellow greasy appearance and is frequently enlarged and inflamed with blubber.

Fatty liver is now acknowledged as one of the most common cause of abnormal liver function assessment results in the States, Great Britain and Australia. Around one in five individuals in the general population, in the U.S.A and Australia has a fatty liver organ. Fatty liver is usually linked to abdominal obesity, insulin resistance and type 2 diabetes. If extreme, it can ultimately lead to liver failure.

How would you know if you have a fatty liver?

Lots of people with a fatty liver are unaware that they even have a liver problem, as the symptoms can be obscure and non-specific, especially in the beginning. Most people with a fatty liver feel typically unwell, and find they are becoming progressively fatigued and overweight for no apparent reason.

Likely symptoms of fatty liver include:

- Weight excess in the abdominal area
- Elevated cholesterol and triglyceride levels
- Tiredness and weakness
- Vomiting
- Gallstones
- Heating up of the system
- Excessive perspiration
- Red itchy eyes

Fortunately fatty liver is reversible:

1. Eat less carbohydrate

Poor diet is the leading root cause of fatty liver disease. The most significant culprits are sugar and foods made of white flour; they need to be kept away from entirely. However, a high intake of carbohydrate rich foods in general can promote fatty liver, as the liver organ converts unwanted starch into fat. Foods that have to be limited consist of bread, pasta, rice, breakfast grains, white potatoes and any food items made of flour.

2. Stop Drinking

Excessive alcohol use is the 2nd greatest cause of fatty liver. Alcohol can easily trigger irritation and harm to liver cells, leading to fatty infiltration.

Stop drinking ... I don't mean cut down. I mean quit drinking completely!

3. Eat more greens, healthy protein and the correct fats

Raw veggies and fruits are the most powerful liver healing foods. These raw foods help to cleanse and restore the liver filtering system, so that it can catch and remove more fat and toxins from the bloodstream. Eat a plethora of vegetables (cooked and raw salads). Fruit is healthy for most people, but if you have elevated blood sugar or insulin resistance, it's optimal to limit fruit to 2 servings daily. Protein is essential because it helps to keep the blood sugar level stable, aids with weight reduction from the abdomen and decreases hunger and cravings. Healthy protein should be consumed with every meal. Good sources of healthy protein include eggs, poultry, seafood, beef, nuts, seeds, whey protein powder, vegetables and milk products.

Most vegetable oil and margarines can worsen a fatty liver. Healthy fats to include more of in your diet are found in olive oil, oily fish, flaxseeds, coconut oil and raw nuts and seeds.

4. Drink raw vegetable juices

Raw juices are an excellent source of very concentrated vitamins, minerals and anti-oxidants. Your fruit juice should be comprised of 80 to 90 percent vegetables, with the remainder comprised of fruit. Do not drink store bought fruit juice; it is too high in carbs and sugar calories.

5. Take a good liver tonic

Choose a liver tonic that incorporates the clinically proven dose of milk thistle with B group vitamins, antioxidants and sulfur rich amino acids. A good liver organ tonic can promote repair of damaged liver cells and help with the fat burning and detoxification abilities of the liver organ.

Extra tip: Boost glutathione production

Glutathione is your liver's most effective detoxifier and it is firmly anti-inflammatory. If you have a fatty liver you need more of it. N-acetyl cysteine is a precursor of glutathione and is understood to increase blood levels strongly. Eating sulfur abundant meals also helps with glutathione; examples include eggs, cabbage, broccoli and garlic.

"People often say that motivation doesn't last. Neither does bathing. That's why we recommend it daily." – Zig Ziglar

When I write a blog article about stopping drinking, there is always at least one person who objects, stating that quitting drinking without medical supervision is lethal.

This is a significant subject and before we get into it, let me give you a disclaimer. I am not a doctor, and I do not offer medical advice. I am a former problem drinker who has helped many thousands of people to escape the trap of daily drinking.

Before you make any significant changes to your lifestyle, you should, of course, consult a GP.

All that said, there is an essential distinction between the stereotypical alcoholic you see portrayed on TV and in the movies. And the type of functional alcoholic that ends up at the Stop Drinking Expert website.

Most people who are addicted to alcohol are not so hooked that they can no longer function in society. They are not the disheveled hoboes you see sitting on a park bench swigging cheap brandy from a bottle hidden inside a brown paper bag.

End-stage alcoholics are entirely debilitated by their drug addiction. They can't go more than a few hours without a drink. For this reason, they can no longer hold down a job, provide for their family, or drive a car. Their whole life has been taken over by their addiction.

These people virtually never end up on my website mainly because they are not functional enough to decide that on their own.

Alcoholics of this nature are not suitable for my approach to alcohol addiction. They are way past the sort of help that I can offer – they need urgent inpatient medical care.

It is true that if someone this addicted to alcohol stopped cold turkey, they would suffer terrible withdrawal, and may even die without medical intervention.

However, this is not a reason for people to keep drinking. The myth that cold turkey = instant death is a fear that is propagated by the alcohol manufacturers and other problem drinkers. The alcohol producers operate deviously and dishonestly just the same way the cigarette manufacturers do.

Alcoholic beverage companies fund research, propaganda, and marketing that spread 'fake news' (I hate that I just used that phrase). Such stories as 'red wine is good for your heart,' 'moderate drinkers live longer than nondrinkers' and of course 'cold turkey is dangerous.' All these are 100% proof bullshit in most cases.

Most people who discover the Stop Drinking Expert website are entirely functioning drinkers. They are good parents, partners, and successful career people. Many have never missed a day of work because of their drinking, and their driving license is clear of DUI's.

My members are not weak-willed, broken, or uneducated. Actually, I have found precisely the opposite tends to be true. The vast majority of my members are incredibly intelligent and successful individuals.

My members are not getting up each morning and reaching for the whiskey bottle. However, they probably are drinking between one and two bottles of wine every night. Despite the propaganda being drip-fed into a society that suggests this level of drinking is risk-free. I can tell you from experience if you sustain this level of drinking for several years, you start to experience devastating consequences.

This level of drinking dramatically affects your finances, health, relationships, and career. Most people drinking to this level feel completely out of control. They wake up every morning, wracked with guilt and regret. Despite how miserable alcohol is making them, they simply can't stop drinking it!

For these people stopping drinking will not cause them to drop down dead suddenly. Their withdrawal experience is mostly insignificant. Often no more than a mild sensation of anxiety and perhaps a few sleepless nights.

The chemical withdrawal from alcohol takes a couple of weeks. This unpleasant but entirely bearable sensation reaches a climax around 24-36 hours after quitting and then slowly fades over the following 14 days.

If your drinking pattern fits the functioning alcoholic description, I have just given then withdrawal is not a reason to continue drinking, sorry!

If you experience any physical symptoms such as trembling and vomiting etc. then, of course, your first course of action should be to visit your GP. Even in these rare cases, it isn't a license to carry on drinking. The doctor will give you some medication to make the physical withdrawal symptoms more tolerable, so you can continue the process.

The alcohol manufacturers are hiding their secret and devious mission under the gloss of expensive and carefully designed marketing. Don't fall for it!

Warning that cold turkey is dangerous may appear at first glance to be a caring advisory, but there is more to it than that. Telling someone who is addicted to a drug that if they stop, they will die makes them feel stressed and anxious.

Guess what people addicted to alcohol turn to when they feel stressed… yes that's right – they drink!

"Learn to enjoy every minute of your life. Be happy now. Don't wait for something outside of yourself to make you happy in the future. Think how really precious is the time you have to spend, whether it's at work or with your family. Every minute should be enjoyed and savored", Earl Nightingale

I received an email the other day from a lady who had been drinking dangerous amounts of alcohol for decades. She was completely broken by the drug; it had made her beyond miserable. Like most problem drinkers she woke every morning full of guilt, shame and regret that yet again it was another hung-over morning.

She stated that more than anything she wanted this poison out of her life but she tempered that by adding 'is it too late, I am 60 next month after all'?

Now, you already know that I am going to say that it isn't too late, but there are some very good reasons why!

Firstly, there is an underlying assumption in such a statement that your twilight years are useless. All I can say to that is when I was fifteen years old I considered people in their forties to be very old indeed. However, now I am one of them I can tell you that I am the happiest and most peaceful that I have ever been. When I was a younger man I was full of rebellion, anger and selfishness.

The truth is you spend the first half of your life building an ego and the second half trying to get away from it. Age brings an new perspective and a wisdom that you can't appreciate until you get there.

Alcohol tricks it's addicts into believe that it is their best friend. It suggests that 'if you think life is bad now, imagine how bad it could be if you removed your only pleasure.

Alcohol is not your best friend; it is your worst enemy. Surely anyone could see that a friend who tells you that your future is going to be crap so you might as well keep taking a lethal drug is actually not friend at all.

Alcohol is a depressant they say, but I prefer to tell people that it is a mood amplifier. If you are having a great time in a nightclub and you also drink alcohol I am willing to admit you can have a lot of fun.

However, when you get addicted to a drug life becomes hard. Alcohol steals so much from you that it becomes increasingly difficult to feel positive. So now you are drinking a mood enhancer on a daily basis when you feel depressed. Suddenly the drink that had the power to make a party go with a swing now has the power to drag you down deeper and deeper every day.

Getting addicted to alcohol is like getting stuck in quick sand. Slowly it takes hold and relentlessly pulls you under. By the time you realize you are in trouble, it doesn't matter how hard you fight – you are going under.

From the point of view of your liver, there is never a point where it's too late to stop drinking. Okay so that's not entirely true, of course there is one point where it's too late. However, if you've already reached that point I would suggest there are better things to do with your remaining time than wonder if you should stop drinking.

Your liver is an amazing organ with the power and will to repair itself. If you can just stop pouring poison into your system for long enough your liver will get to work on mopping up a lot of the damage that has been done over the years.

Think about it, imagine if you knew with totally certainty that you would die in ten years time. Would you want to spend your last decade in poor health, feeling tired and miserable, broke and addicted to a drug that knocks you out and robs you of your precious remaining time. Or would you want to spend ten years living life to the max. Spending quality time with the people you love and not sat in a hospital waiting room?

Everyday you put alcohol in your mouth you gift it another 24 hours of your precious life. I know that if you only had 24 hours left you wouldn't want to spend it a sleep on the sofa with a bottle of whiskey in your hand.

The ego loves alcohol because it encourages this sort of negative thinking. Alcohol uses the power of the conscious mind to create compelling (if entirely erroneous) reasons to carry on drinking. But you should know that the ego operates entirely in two time periods that don't exist.

The ego lives in the past and the future, never in the present moment. It will suggest to you that the past was a better time to be in and the future can only be worse. This is why the saying goes 'if you want to be sad, live in the past. If you want to be worried, live in the future'. The only time that exists and will ever exist is now and it is a beautiful gift – that's why they call it the present.

To suggest it is 'too late to stop drinking' implies that you know for sure when you are going to shuffle off this mortal coil. This is something nobody gets to know in advance.

Two days ago there was a terrorist attack in London and a 30 year old Canadian woman called Christine Archibald died in the arms of her fiancé. Nobody could have predicted that and she couldn't have known that her beautiful life would be stolen at such a young age.

Equally the 60-year-old woman who inspired this chapter with her question could feasibly live another 60 years. She will never know until the present moment catches up.

It doesn't matter what has gone before and we have no idea what is coming in the future. This is why I tell my stop drinking expert members to not count the days since they had a drink. Equally I advise people to stop thinking about an entire lifetime without a drink. You may or may not get an entire lifetime, so the only time you need to worry about is now.

Be grateful that in this precise moment you are not drinking attractively packaged poison for fun. Seriously, yes the best time for her to have stopped drinking was twenty years ago. However, the next best time is right now!

"Temptation is like a knife, that may either cut the meat or the throat of a man; it may be his food or his poison, his exercise or his destruction", John Owen

If you went on a weight loss diet you probably wouldn't fill the fridge with cakes and chocolate right?

Alcohol is slightly different but temptation can still be a problem.

One of the biggest problems that people face when quitting drinking is where they have a partner or other significant member of the household who also drinks to excess.

In a perfect world you would both address the problem together and make the sound decision to push this poison out of your relationship entirely. However, that is a rare and unusual situation.

Normally one person in the house wakes up and realized how much damage is being done by the booze but their partner wants to continue drinking. So, how do you stay sober in a house full of alcohol?

First it is worth mentioning that some ex drinking individuals are so committed to their sobriety that they have no issue with alcohol being in the home.

I have previously been in relationships with people who drank alcohol and their home featured the usual wine rack and bottle of half drunk sherry in the cupboard. At no point was I tempted to drink the stuff and after a while I didn't even notice it. It was a bit like an ornament – you notice it initially but then it just becomes a part of the background.

Nonetheless, quitting any sort of drug addiction is a noble but challenging decision. You deserve to have your choice respected and to expect those that love you to support and encourage your sobriety.

If you were trying to kick heroin into touch it would be considered highly irresponsible and selfish behavior for other members of the home to bring the drug (and use it in front of you) into the house.

However, despite killing a person every 90 seconds and being the second most addictive drug on planet earth. Alcohol has special permission to be viewed as a harmless social pleasantry. Alcohol has managed to twist reality so aggressively that it is the people who don't use the drug who are considered to be strange.

I believe it is reasonable to ask members of your household to support your decision to quit drinking by not having any alcohol in the home. Ideally this would be a permanent choice, and I will explain why in a moment. However, I understand it is difficult to achieve this utopia when you live with other people who are addicted to alcohol and unwilling to address the issue. In these cases try to agree a three or six month period when no alcohol will be allowed in the house.

This sort of time period will allow you to go through the chemical kick from the drug and establish some new routines and patterns. Alcohol has taken up a lot of your time in the past and it takes a while to work out what you are going to do with all this free time. There will be moments where you are bored, restless and don't know what to do with yourself.

Don't forget, you are used to drinking an anesthetic each evening. You have conditioned yourself to believe that being in a foggy, zombie-like haze is normal. When you quit drinking you may be shocked by how much more energy you have – this can actually feel a little unsettling initially.

If your partner refuses to remove alcohol from the home, this may be an indicator of how significant their own problem with alcohol has become. Couples who drink together tend to both bury their head in the sand and collectively choose to avoid the issue. Of course you can't force your partner to comply with your wishes, but if they won't then you should use this as further motivation. This is pure evidence of how deeply alcohol has infected your relationship and it may lead to bigger more challenging conversations in the future.

Why the ideal situation is not to have alcohol in the home:

My partner Daniela drinks, but extremely rarely. I think in the last year I have seen her have no more than 3 glasses of wine. When we moved in together she had a couple of bottle of spirits, purely stuff to offer guests when the came calling.

While I was not worried I would be tempted to drink them, I asked her if she would mind if we threw them away and had an alcohol free house. She agreed and it really does make a huge difference.

Our home is a place of love and family. It is where we spend time together, where we eat, laugh, talk and enjoy our relationship. When you have something malignant in the home I believe it's presence leaks into the atmosphere of the house. I wouldn't feel comfortable having a gun in the house and I don't feel comfortable having addictive drugs in the house.

That may make me sound like a wishy washy new age type but I can tell you from experience. When you live in a household where alcohol never appears in any form you feel significantly more peaceful and happy.

Does Alcohol Cause Arthritis?

"Without health life is not life; it is only a state of langour and suffering - an image of death", Buddha

'Cause' is probably the wrong word in this question because it is almost a certainty that alcohol is not the trigger for the onset of rheumatoid arthritis. Perhaps the more relevant question is 'does alcohol aggravate arthritis'?

When it comes to RA the current thinking about alcohol is significantly different from that of smoking. We know for certain that tobacco use directly accelerates the progress of the disease. Almost certainly you will be advised to stop smoking if you are diagnosed with arthritis.

The water is somewhat cloudier when it comes to alcohol. Many people claim that drinking in moderation actually helps with the pain and symptoms of rheumatoid arthritis. This is not entirely a surprise because alcohol is a mild anesthetic. If you have any condition that involves pain in the body then it should be obvious that taking a substance that numbs the central nervous system is going to be seen in a positive light.

Using alcohol as medication is never a good idea. This is why when someone is rushed to hospital in cardiac arrest the doctors never put him or her on a Merlot drip… Stat! This is despite all the claims that red wine is good for our hearts.

Equally GP's don't prescribe alcohol for pain management. The side effects far outweigh the benefits, plus alcohol is the second most addictive substance on planet earth. Prescribing alcohol to deal with pain would be like sawing off your leg to stop your foot hurting.

However, all that said – alcohol in small amounts does not seem to aggravate arthritis in most people. Good news you may think, but as always there is a little more depth to the story.

In my book Escaping The Evil Clown I refer to booze as the ultimate magician. It is always distracting you with impressive sleight of hand to keep your attention away from what is really going on.

Alcohol has you focus on the good times, the illusion of relaxation and many other faux benefits to stop you noticing the addiction taking root.

Alcoholism and rheumatoid arthritis are similar, but only in that they are both progressive diseases. They will both get worse given time, never better. If you drink and have arthritis you are unwittingly creating a perfect storm for your future self.

The more you drink alcohol the more you are going to get addicted – this is an unmistakable fact. Your arthritis is going to get worse over time, not because of the booze but just because of the nature of the disease. At some point it will become so painful and debilitating that you are going to go to the doctor and ask for prescription drugs to help.

The GP will no doubt oblige and prescribe you anti inflammatory pain relief (NSAIDS) and possibly a new disease modifying anti rheumatic drug (DMARD) like methotrexate.

All these drugs require you to either stop drinking or severely limited your alcohol consumption. However, this is a problem for the drinker because by now they are so hooked on booze that they can't quit.

What this means is the painkillers will lose a great deal of their effectiveness because of their interaction with alcohol. This means you will be in much more pain than you need to be.

However, there is another problem. Drugs like methotrexate are metabolized in the liver just like alcohol. If you mix these DMARD's with alcohol very bad things start to happen.

Your liver which has been under attack from the alcohol now has another toxin to deal with. But worse than that, the whole becomes far greater than the sum of the parts. Alcohol mixed with methotrexate is like moving from attacking you liver with conventional weapons to pulling out the big guns and dropping nukes.

So to summarize: alcohol does not cause arthritis, it does not even trigger a flare up. However, getting addicted to alcohol is going to cause you huge problems in the future.

How to master sobriety and really embrace teetotalism.

"The more aware of your intentions and your experiences you become, the more you will be able to connect the two, and the more you will be able to create the experiences of your life consciously. This is the development of mastery. It is the creation of authentic power", Gary Zukav

If you want to be a success in life then the advice is to model yourself and your habits on those of others who have achieved success. It is no coincidence that most millionaire entrepreneurs have very similar routines and disciplines in life.

Vladimir Putin is an individual who has been in the media quite a lot of late. Regardless of how the western press portrays him, back home in Russia he is revered and respected. In the UK Theresa May attempted to appear 'strong and stable' by simply repeating the phrase as the answer to any question she was asked. Of course it failed, because the general public are not as stupid as career politicians assume.

Putin owns 'strong and stable' in Russia because he has a set of principles that he won't compromise on. These include a daily two-hour swim, a ban on all technology in his office and a solid commitment to teetotalism.

Part of the reason he doesn't drink is to send a message to the public that alcohol is not necessary or advisable. This is a part of his belief structure and I doubt you will ever catch him with a drink in his hand.

The difference between people who successfully kick alcohol out of their life and those that don't is largely down to mindset and how much passion they have for what they are doing.

In the years of running StopDrinkingExpert.com I have noticed that the people who really manage to escape this drug are the ones who get a little bit obsessed with what they are doing. Living a sober life becomes an essential part of their being. Sobriety becomes woven into the fabric of their outlook; it's as much a part of them as their views on fidelity, friendship and family.

In a way they embrace teetotalism just as passionately as some people take to veganism. It doesn't mean they are never tempted to have the odd bacon sandwich but their beliefs are so firmly embedded that it never gets any further than just that 'the odd temptation'.

The frustration for me as an alcohol therapist is watching people repeatedly trying to use willpower to stop drinking. I see many comments along the lines of 'managed to get through the weekend without a drink' and 'damn, I was doing so well and then I buckled last night and had a beer or two'.

These comments are followed up by well meaning people who say 'don't beat yourself up, you did well to last a week' etc.

Let me be absolutely clear about this 'you did not do well to last a week'. You have failed to understand the way alcohol works. The drug is more than happy for you to go a week without a drink, because it knows you will come back to it even harder every time you do this.

Once you get truly committed to living a sober life then there is no 'getting through the weekend'. There is no battle because you are not forcing yourself to avoid something that you want. Vegan's rarely have to say 'thank God the weekend is over, I made it through without having to eat some lovely meat'. Not eating animals is a part of their personality, it is who they are!

Now, of course I know that meat is not addictive and that is where the comparison falls down. However, what I am trying to tell you is, if you are serious about quitting drinking then you need to make teetotalism a part of who you are.

Decades of drinking alcohol has physically altered your brain. Because of this, you can never go back to moderate drinking, ever! From now on when you drink this attractively packaged poison your brain is going to light up like a Christmas tree.

Despite what some people say, your neural pathways will never return to normal.

With this hard reality you have a choice. You can spend the rest of your life being miserable forcing yourself to avoid the thing you want the most (AA style). Or you can reframe alcohol so it becomes as repugnant to you as a leather jacket is to a committed vegan.

When you are planning your sober recovery from this drug you need to be on your guard for the lies that your addiction will tell you. All these negative beliefs come from f.e.a.r. (False Evidence Appearing Real). For example, many people come to the conclusion that they have an addictive personality and therefore their drinking is not their fault.

They may curse their parents or the medical community, anyone but themselves or their drug. Once you start pointing the finger of blame at an external source you fall into the trap of the drug.

Nobody is to blame for your addiction to alcohol, including yourself. However, you are entirely responsible for dealing with it. Nobody is going to come in and fix this issue for you. Sure, you can get advice and information to make your journey out of the loop easier. But at the end of the day it is only you who can implement and commit to a sober recovery plan.

In reality there is no such thing as an 'addictive personality'. If drinkers all shared such a kink in character then all drinkers would look, act and behave in a similar way. However, attend any rehab clinic and look around at the clients. You will find a completely diverse mix of individuals.

Alcohol hooks all races, genders and social classes. It doesn't care where you live, how many children you have or how powerful you are. Kings and paupers alike are fair game for this drug.

If it really were possible to have an addictive personality then these poor individuals would be addicted to everything. All alcoholics afflicted with this condition would also weigh 400lbs from all the candy they were addicted to. They would be smoking 40 cigarettes a day while sniffing glue constantly.

The moment you come up with a reason to explain your drinking you have a license to fail. Accept no explanation, no reason and no justification. Take responsibility for killing the Evil Clown yourself alone.

What does dreaming about drinking alcohol mean after quitting?

"Every great dream begins with a dreamer. Always remember, you have within you the strength, the patience, and the passion to reach for the stars to change the world", Harriet Tubman

There were many things about my drinking behavior that I thought were unique to me. Then when I eventually quit drinking poison for fun I also believed that my experiences of quitting were also unique.

However, when I started to write about these things I was shocked to find so many people getting in touch to say that they also experienced the same things.

Many have said 'it is like you reached inside my head and told my own story'.

Alcohol twists reality so profoundly that we assume that it can only be us going through this insanity. Our propensity to follow social proof makes us believe that other people are somehow better at coping with this addiction than us.

During the decade that I was aware that my drinking was dangerously out of control but still didn't want to give it up. I did some ridiculously absurd things to try and prove that I wasn't an alcoholic.

As it turns out, I am not alone. I have discovered there are some entirely predictable elements to alcohol addiction. Dealing with thousands of people struggling with their drinking has taught me how to predict what they will experience next.

This has been powerfully helpful because when I see someone struggling I can understand what is going through his or her mind. I have heard every excuse going and I can spot drinkers bullshit from a mile away.

I won't lie to you, there are parts of my stop drinking program that are difficult and challenging. Certainly during the first two weeks you have both chemical and psychological addiction to deal with. That can be tough if your mindset is not 100% right.

However, there are also elements that are more confusing than difficult. Dreaming about drinking alcohol is certainly one of them. Firstly, you need to be aware that you are not alone and it is common.

Secondly, don't worry it's not a bad thing – quite the contrary.

Many of my members wake up in a blind panic a week or so after stopping drinking. They have had a dream that they were drinking and it was so vivid and real that they are not even sure it was just a dream.

This also happened to me. I am not sure why the dreams are so vivid and lucid but I woke up many times after quitting drinking and actually searched through the garbage to make sure that I really didn't drink the night before.

I also often woke up with a terrible hangover despite not having had a drop of alcohol. This always struck me as being super unfair – to get the punishment without committing the crime.

What I can say to any drinker who is newly sober and is dealing with these issues is. It is exactly what happened to me, and if you continue to follow the same route that I did. You will end up happily sober for the rest of your life.

Why Does It Happen?

Dreaming is important for your physical and mental health. Your subconscious is an amazing machine and it never sleeps. After you have been visited by the sandman and are in a deep, colorful dream. Your subconscious is problem solving and correctly filing the vast amount of data you absorbed during the day.

By the time you develop a problem with alcohol, it has been a significant part of your life for decades. Because you are programmed at a genetic level to stay alive as long as possible, your system has miraculously adapted as best it can to having poison in your blood 24/7.

Alcohol has become a constant part of your life. When you remove it, there are parts of you that don't understand what's happening. Suddenly everything feels different, your brain is no longer operating with a sedative on board, and everything seems sharper and clearer.

Change anything this significant in your life and your body is initially going to object and take a little time to adjust to the new reality. Your subconscious is trying to make sense of what has happened. You experience this through your dreams.

Example:

If you are used to driving on the left hand side of the road and you travel to a country that drives on the right. Initially you feel very uncomfortable and panicked. Everything feels disorientating and in the wrong place. But after a few days you adapt and it becomes a subconscious routine.

This is similar to what is happening with the removal of alcohol but on a much more significant scale.

How long will it last?

How long is a piece of string? Some people never experience anything like this and others will have drinking dreams for months.

Personally I experienced drinking dreams quite regularly for about a month. Then slowly they reduced in frequency until I had the last one I remember, about seven months out from my last drink.

The phantom hangovers lasted about the same length of time but with much less frequency than the dreams of drinking alcohol. Those crazy nightmares that would wake me up in a panic that I had gone back to the booze.

Don't be worried by them and don't assume it is a sign that you are going to return to drinking. It is purely a part of the detoxification process where your body has to get used to living without constant poison in your blood stream. This is a very good thing.

Is Alcohol Use Disorder Different to Alcoholism?

"Life is a sexually transmitted disease and the mortality rate is one hundred percent", R. D. Laing

Alcohol Use Disorder (AUD) is a new and increasingly popular term used to describe the misuse of alcohol.

The phrase is being used progressively by celebrities and seems to cover all use of alcohol as a coping mechanism. For example, if you use alcohol to a daily basis to get to sleep or to relax then you would fit the criteria of the label.

I believe AUD became a thing purely because people don't like the word alcoholic, especially career or status minded individuals. I completely understand this position. Back when I was a drinker I refused to label myself as an alcoholic because I didn't believe I fit the stereotype.

I wasn't missing work, getting driving violations or sitting in the park swigging whiskey from a brown paper bag. Even today, as I have previously mentioned I don't use the term alcoholic to describe my addiction.

While I understand the reasons for coming up with a more palatable phrase. I also believe there is danger in doing so!

Alcohol Use Disorder is the sort of wording that implies that it is an unavoidable condition such as autism. It almost suggests that the sufferer of the condition was just very unfortunate some how.

"Hey did you hear about Dave, poor guy's only gone and caught AUD".

I get that nobody wants to get a reputation for being an alcoholic but to come up with a more digestible label may dissociate people from the true cause (and solution) of their issue.

With any addiction the primary obstacle is always denial. You have to admit that a problem exists before you have any hope of addressing it.

At least a few times a week someone will approach me with concerns about the drinking of a close friend or family member. They want to know what they can do to help them cut down or quit drinking completely.

The first question I always ask is 'do they admit they have a problem'. Followed by 'do they want to stop drinking'. Answering either question with no will invariably mean you can't do anything to help them at the moment.

People who don't want to stop drinking don't! You can't force them or trick them into it.

So if people are using the term Alcohol Use Disorder to protect their reputation while they are busy dealing with the problem then I see no issue. However, if they are claiming to have AUD purely to throw a pity party and validate their drinking behavior then the consequences should be obvious.

I am not applying blame to anyone here; I am not saying people are at fault for their drinking problems. The nature of the drug is to get you hooked. Getting addicted shouldn't be considered to be unusual or an indicator of weakness.

Alcohol is addictive, very addictive. If you drink it long enough you will develop a problem – this much is inevitable. However, dealing with it effectively always means taking 100% responsibility for it.

No matter what label you choose to give yourself – you created this problem by repeatedly drinking an addictive drug. Only you can fix the problem by the actions you take next.

My advice to people who are concerned about their drinking is; don't get hung up on labels. Focus your energy and passion on the solution to your problem rather than the explanation for it being there in the first place.

There should be no indignity in admitting you have a problem with alcohol. Smokers don't have to hang their head in shame and admit that they were previously addicted to nicotine.

Ex-smokers are often praised for kicking the habit. Meanwhile ex-drinkers are still approached with a certain amount of pity and sympathy.

This will change, and so it should but I suspect it will take time. We are only seeing the very tip of the alcoholism iceberg at the moment.

You don't need a label to deal with this… just deal with it!

Does life without alcohol suck?

"Today I choose life. Every morning when I wake up I can choose joy, happiness, negativity, pain... To feel the freedom that comes from being able to continue to make mistakes and choices - today I choose to feel life, not to deny my humanity but embrace it", Kevyn Aucoin

This question came from a couple of my Stop Drinking program members who were chatting on Facebook. They were agreeing with each other that a life without alcohol appears to be dull.

I can completely understand this thinking. I probably spent five years of my drinking life avoiding dealing with my addiction due the same sort of thinking.

Alcohol was so deeply ingrained into my life that I simply couldn't see how I could function without it. I worried that I would have no way to relax, no way to socialize and even no way to get to sleep of a night.

The only thing I can tell you, having been on both sides of the coin is this. The worry that life is less without alcohol is just another illusion of the drug.

You have to marvel at the power of this poison. It has the power to make you look at black and call it white. Alcohol brings nothing but misery and suffering and yet somehow it manages to persuade you that you can't live without it.

I wish I had the words to describe the difference between my happy sober life now and the fat, zombified existence that I insisted I 'enjoyed' as a drunk.

It's a frustrating problem for me personally, because I speak for a living. I spent over twenty years as a professional broadcaster and yet I can't describe just how much better my life is without alcohol. Perhaps the words don't exist!

I have mentioned repeatedly about the obvious downsides of alcohol addiction. The fact that it steals your money, time, health and relationships.

What I have never talked about before is the damage alcohol does to your spiritual health.

Wait… before you run away because I have gone all-spiritual on you. What I mean by spiritual is a inner state of peace and happiness. We as a species get a little confused between happiness and fun. I believe happiness comes from within and fun is just an external input.

Whether you are religious, spiritual or just open to meditation the fundamental goal remains the same: To reduce the ego and spend more time in grateful appreciation of the present moment. True peace and happiness only exists in the 'now', never in the future or past.

Alcohol prevents you achieving this aim. The alcohol addict is rarely in the moment. While they are consuming alcohol they are sedated and prevented from being fully aware by the drug. When they are not drinking they are plotting and planning when they will next be able to do so.

I recorded a video to go along with this chapter. I went to the beach where I got married fifteen years ago. The stunningly beautiful location I have been with my children and family many times in the past.

Until I went back to make the video I can honestly say I have never really been there before. Let me explain that statement, sure I have been there physically, many times before. However, I was never really present mentally to appreciate the beauty around me.

All I was thinking was 'yes very good, when can we go back to the hotel'. It's not that the hotel was so amazing that I couldn't bare to be parted from it. I think you know why I was so desperate to get back to the hotel.

Finally when I stood on that beach sober and allowed myself to really experience the beauty of the place, a wave of peace washed over me. It almost brought a tear to my eye – a powerful moment I allowed alcohol to steal from me a million times over.

If you want to be sad live in the past, if you want to be worried live in the future. Happiness and true peace exists only in the present moment.

Alcohol will do everything it can to prevent you staying here.

What you will find is that after six months of sober living, you will look back on the question of whether 'life without alcohol sucks' and laugh until you are sick.

There is nothing I can say to really persuade a drinker of this, all I can do is challenge you to experience it. I know you will come back to me full of shock, excitement and pure joy having experienced first hand what a sober life feels like.

How do you stop thinking about drinking alcohol?

"When you begin to worry, go find something to do. Get busy being a blessing to someone; do something fruitful. Talking about your problem or sitting alone, thinking about it, does no good; it serves only to make you miserable. Above all else, remember that worrying is totally useless. Worrying will not solve your problem", Joyce Meyer

When you get addicted to alcohol a lot of things change and a lot of strange behaviors become normal to you. Drinkers think about alcohol all the time.

If they are not drinking the stuff they are planning when they can next. Addicts are constantly risk assessing every situation in life to make sure alcohol will be available should they want to drink.

This scary level of obsessive behavior becomes commonplace. But you only have to change the substance for the insanity to become obvious. Imagine if over a hundred times a day you though about potatoes.

When you weren't eating them you were planning where you can get your next fix of potato. If your friend invited you to a party and you found out that there would be no potatoes available. This would lead to a major tantrum and your refusal to attend.

If you were behaving like that around the humble spud on a daily basis. It wouldn't be long before your friends suggested medical intervention.

The human body is an amazing thing. It will physically adapt and change to better perform tasks that you do on a regular basis.

For example in you decided to switch your writing hand, your body would eventually adapt to this change. After a decade of writing only with your left hand instead of the right you would find it strange and difficult to go back.

The same is true of habits and addictions. For decades you have been thinking about alcohol on a daily basis. Your mind expects this routine to be a part of your reality. So, don't be surprised if it doesn't stop as dramatically as you would perhaps prefer.

When you first quit drinking you will find alcohol or the lack of it is still on your mind often. This slowly fades away but it will never go away completely.

A couple of days ago I stayed in a hotel I have not been to for over a decade. The last time I was there I remember checking in and getting the room key. But instead of going straight to the room I went out of the hotel to a convenience store. I bought a bag of chips and a huge bottle of Ouzo, which I planned to drink in the room.

This time I did head straight to the room after check in. However, as soon as my foot crossed the threshold into the hotel suite, I had a powerful sensation come over me. I suddenly thought 'should I go an buy some Ouzo'?

Of course as soon as I had the thought, I dismissed it as a terrible idea. However, you should be aware that even when you have been sober as long as me – these crazy thoughts still appear.

Some people get a little despondent about these sorts of thoughts. They worry that these mind farts are a sign that they have not really beaten the drug.

As with everything else in life you can't change the things you are not in control of. You can only change the way you respond to them.

For example, getting upset at the law of gravity won't make any difference to how it affects your body.

Instead of getting upset or angry when these thoughts occur, see them as a positive. They are little reminders that alcohol wants to pull you back in to the trap.

Alcohol is like a little demon, you have not beaten him, you have locked him in a little box. He can't hurt you as long as you keep the box locked.

Occasionally he will shout out and beg you to put the key in the lock and give him a little air. Just like feeding a Gremlin after midnight, answering his plea is going to end in nothing but pain and misery for you.

Don't punish yourself for having these thoughts and don't feel bad about them. If you try and push them away or demand that they don't ever appear you actually make them stronger and more regular. Instead, when they appear, just acknowledge them, watch them unfold before you and then let them go.

"A culture that denies death inevitably becomes shallow and superficial, concerned only with the external form of things. When death is denied, life loses its depth", Eckhart Tolle

Alcohol is treated as the go to panacea for all of life's major curve balls. Lose your job, get dumped by a partner or even suffer the agony of bereavement. You can be assured that a well-meaning friend or relative will reach straight for a stiff drink.

When people consider giving up booze for good there are many social aspects of the drug that they worry they will miss out on. But also it is common to be concerned that a coping mechanism will also be lost out on.

On the 4th July 2017 my ex-wife and mother of my two wonderful children died suddenly and unexpectedly. She was not ill, not a risk taker and only fifty years of age. Our world crashed down around us and for me personally the most difficult part of the whole horrible ordeal was watching my children suffer and not be able to do anything to pull them out of their torture.

You may wonder if at any point in this painful experience if I was tempted to drink. The honest answer is yes.

The days between Denise's death and the funeral felt intolerably long. Every minute felt like a week. As we waited for family and friends to fly in from around the world I woke every morning and tried desperately to fill the days with distractions for my children.

On the third day they were both visiting friends and I was left on my own in a hotel room for a good eight hours. I didn't want to be on my own and I didn't want my stupid brain to keep replaying events over and over again.

I briefly considered walking to a liquor store and buying a bottle of whiskey. The thought lasted no more than a few seconds before I quickly recognized that life was already hard enough without adding another problem.

Alcohol would have just made a bad situation worse. Plus, what I have learnt well in the past is; once you invite the monkey onto your back, he won't let go for a very long time. You will have to wrestle with him and prize his gnarled, devilishly strong fingers from your flesh one by one.

I believe that the vast majority of the drinkers I meet are intelligent individuals who are simply using alcohol to escape the harsh edges of life.

Get an unexpected bill – drink it away.
Mess things up at work – drink it away.
Miss out on the promotion – drink it away.
Argue with your partner – drink it away.

However, as I explain in Alcohol Lied to Me; booze doesn't fast forward you through stressful or painful events. It may appear that is what it is doing but in reality it just hits the pause button on life. When the drug wears off you are presented with the original problem but now you have an additional issue to deal with. That being, the withdrawal from a highly addictive drug.

In the case of my own personal experience recently. Grief has a natural process and as painful as it is you can't choose to skip any part of it.

My son is nineteen now but still very much a baby at heart. He absolutely adored his mother and he took her death very hard indeed. I had with me some prescription sedatives, but no matter how much he struggled with what was happening I resisted the urge to give him a tablet.

Experiencing the agony of the first four stages of grief are the only true route to the fifth and final phase, which is that of acceptance. Sedation would only delay that journey further.

The same is true of alcohol. You can drink and zombify yourself for a while but you can't cheat the system. The piper will have to be paid sooner or later. Nobody in their right mind would choose to pay later and extend the misery a second longer than is needed.

Once you get to the point where you accept that sobriety is a part of whom you are. Then you will start to feel immensely grateful in the dark times that you don't also have alcohol addiction to deal with.

You don't get a choice on this. Life is going to knock you down repeatedly; it is the nature of existence. Getting back up again is the only true choice. Getting back up sober is so much quicker and easier than trying to do so with a booze monkey clinging around your neck.

Alcohol addiction is similar to getting stuck in quicksand. In both cases, we make an inaccurate assessment of the risk and the situation. We tend to only address our drinking when we have already started sinking up to our waist. You will notice that in areas where quicksand is a possibility they do not put up the warning signs in the middle of the danger. They put them right out there on the perimeter, long before you get near the danger zone.

The same is true of alcohol. When you first take a sip of booze and discover to your shock that it tastes vile. This should be an alarm bell that scares us off for life. However, we take a look around and notice that everyone else is drinking and apparently enjoying their alcoholic drink. So we persevere despite all the evidence suggesting that drinking horrible tasting poison for fun is at best ill-advised.

So, we learn how to tolerate alcohol and to mix our metaphors, we keep walking towards the center of the quicksand. Then when we realize we are sinking we start to panic and struggle to control our drinking. We use willpower to force ourselves to drink less of the thing we want most in the world. The truth is using willpower to escape an alcohol problem is as misguided a plan as kicking and struggling are as an effective way to get out of quicksand.

The harsh reality is the more you panic the deeper you sink. The more you try to force yourself to go back to being a 'normal or social' drinker of attractively packaged poison the more you experience failure. Constantly failing to achieve your goal leads to low mood and stress. This then accelerates the problem because us drinkers have a solution for times when we are a bit down in the dumps... we drink!

It's very hard to get out of quicksand on your own. Really what you need is someone to come along, spot you are in trouble and reach out a hand to help you out. That is exactly what I do for people like you!

This book is a powerful first step because not least, you have taken action on a problem that the vast majority of people refuse to deal with. However, if you are otherwise a successful individual with a lot to lose then refusing to take that helping hand is a gamble with significant consequences.

Consider what could happen to your career, income, reputation and loved ones if you don't deal with this problem. How would life look like in five years time if your drinking just kept getting worse?

Helping people escape the trap of alcoholism is my passion. If you ever attend one of my quit drinking events you will see just how much I throw into this. I live it and I breathe it. This is why over the years I have gained the reputation as the World's #1 Quit Drinking Mentor. Every year I work with a handful of people on a one to one basis. I effectively become your sponsor. We talk (video) on a regular basis and I make sure you nail this problem once and for all.

This is the most powerful and effective alcohol cessation solution anywhere today.

- Personal mentor calls with Craig Beck
- Custom scripted & recorded hypnosis
- Complete step by step video course
- Secret Facebook group
- Inner circle upgrade
- Non-judgmental community
- Free entry into any live event
- 75 hours video & audio coaching
- 90 days intensive support

- Lifetime access & support

If you are interested in my Executive Quit Drinking Program visit the website and arrange a free consultation with me.

"Life turns on a dime", Stephen King

Nothing happens until something moves, as the saying goes. That something has to be you, nobody else is going to do this for you. I want to close this book by giving you very clear steps to take next.

1. Watch The Movie 'Click'

The objective of this book is not just for you to stop drinking, but also for you to find that your new sober lifestyle delivers with it real happiness. There is no point being sober and miserable. So many people spend their lives ignoring (or drowning out with alcohol) internal alarm bells ringing all over the place. Something inside is trying to tell these people that something vital to their peace and happiness is missing. But rather than deal with this internal void they throw a rug over the hole inside them and pretend it isn't there. Alcohol hides the problem but it doesn't fix it.

Drinking to avoid life is perhaps one of the most common reasons I hear to explain an addiction to alcohol. The problem with using alcohol for this reason is rather than it allowing a person to fast forward through time and consciously delete all the troubles and stresses that are currently pressing (as they believe it does). Drinking actually just hits the pause button on the great CD player of life, in the morning when the anaesthetic has worn off the track begins to play from the precise position it was stopped at the night before. Not a single moment of the misery has been skipped; it has simply been frozen and kept fresh for another time. The great 'Disappearing Time Trick' turns out to be complete bunkum, nothing more than smoke and mirrors. Conned by the dark magician, the drinker now has the compound problem of yesterday's problems to deal with on top of the new challenges that will surely present themselves today.

This function of alcohol reminds me of a very funny (and at times painfully sad) movie starring Adam Sandler called 'Click'. In which an ambitious architect called Michael Newman, played by Sandler makes a deal with the Devil, whereby he is given a universal remote control that not only does all the usual things you would expect from such a device such as turning on the television or opening the garage doors but in addition it can also magically control real life too. Michael quickly realises to his delight that with the click of a button he can fast forward through time and even skip events all together.

He stumbles across this apparently miraculous feature of the remote while shivering in sub zero temperatures waiting for his dog to take a leak before bed. The pooch is quite happy sniffing around the yard, oblivious to the encouragement to 'do his business' coming from his frustrated and freezing owner. Curiously Newman points the remote at the dog and hits the fast forward button. In a blur of activity including the rather repugnant cocking of the leg incident he is left gobsmacked by the awesome power of his new device.

As the story unfolds he uses the remote more and more, skipping arguments with his wife, fast forwarding boring visits from the in-laws and eventually incorrectly assuming he was shortly to be promoted at work he asks the remote to jump forward to the day he makes partner at his firm of architects. What he doesn't realise is his promotion was actually a whole decade away and the remote is an intelligent device that learns the behaviour of its owner and then attempts to predict future.

The remote assumes that because he has skipped such things as sex with his wife, play time with his kids, Christmas and birthday parties that in the future he will also not want to experience them. It then proceeds to ignore his objections and automatically fast forward him through some of the most sacred and special moments in life. Towards the end of the movie we see an aged, ill and overweight Michael Newman who is distraught because he has missed his children growing up, lost his wife to another man and has sold his soul to be the most successful partner in the company. He is desperately unhappy and full of regret at throwing away all the moments that makes life really worth living.

I have watched that movie a dozen times, I must have even seen it four or five times with a big glass of whiskey in my hand completely oblivious to how the universal remote is a metaphor for alcohol.

Alcohol makes a deal with people but like a shady insurance salesman it fails to tell them about the small print. It promises to make their problems disappear and while it does make good on that deal what it doesn't mention until it is too late is that the problems will be back the next day but much bigger than ever before. And just like a gambling addict desperately chasing his losses looking for one big payday, now the original problems are exponentially bigger and more painful. Unable to cope with the avalanche of worry the drinker must now make another significantly larger deal with the devil – the seemingly unbreakable cycle begins in earnest.

2. Catch your ego at work

Become conscious of your ego trying to hijack your thinking. All statements that begin with the word 'I' are a clear indication that the ego is speaking.

For example

- I deserve a drink.
- I can have one drink as a treat.
- I can control my drinking this time.
- I had a hard day, I need a drink to relax.

You will also notice that all these statements come from a position of fear. The word 'deserve' implies that you have suffered and this should be recognised with a reward. The word 'have' suggests that you believe you need an external substance to make you happy and the word 'control' is easily identified as a negative element. The ego speaks from a position of fear. However, your soul (which knows exactly what you need to be healthy and happy) always speaks from a position of love, always! This is the voice you should be listening to.

3. Find your purpose

Many people are using alcohol to cover up a feeling of emptiness within them. If you are not happy with the direction of your life, the quicker you make a course correction the quicker things will start to improve. Alcohol is trapping you on a path that ultimately won't serve you. That nagging voice inside you is there to remind you that you are here for a profound and important reason. That something inside you is trying to motivate you to take action. In the past you have dealt with this nagging sensation by drinking alcohol (a mild anaesthetic) to try and make it go away.

I don't know what it is for you, but there is almost certainly something you enjoy doing so much that when you do it time flies by. Whether this is painting, photography, running your own business or just playing golf – find the thing you are passionate about and do it… a lot! I am also certain that at the moment alcohol is stealing enough of your time to prevent you pursuing this passion of yours.

4. Kick the kick

Be prepared for alcohol to kick and scream like a petulant child when you try to quit. For up to two weeks you may experience mild sensations of anxiety and or stress. These are nothing more than cravings being generated by the drug to try and force you back to the bottle. Remember, the reason why alcohol has the power to kill 3.5 million people every year is its ability to trick otherwise intelligent individuals into consuming attractively packaged poison. Ask yourself what do alcohol dependant people do when they are stressed out? Yes, that's right they drink. The Alcohol Monster knows this and so it will try and induce stress and anxiety in you with the goal of getting you to respond in your usual and predictable way. You may come home from work having had the bitch of all days and believe that you deserve a drink more than anything else. Despite how powerfully and logical it appears, remember what it really is and don't fall for it!

Make sure you have understood the tapping techniques and other craving control strategies we talked about in chapter six. The chemical kick from alcohol is gone after two weeks; things get much easier from this point.

5. Don't lie down with dogs

You are making an important lifestyle decision. This choice is a lot easier if you surround yourself with people who support and encourage you. If you tell your drinking friends that you are thinking of quitting booze they will in all likelihood attempt to sabotage your efforts. This might sound like strange behaviour to expect from people who are supposed to love and care for you. However, what you must remember is alcoholism is a learned addiction. We all had to work very hard over many years to teach ourselves to ignore the horrible taste, painful hangovers and in built knowledge that we are knowingly consuming poison for fun. All drinkers carry a nagging worry that what they are doing must one day stop, but most people respond to this by sticking their fingers in their ears to block out this painful truth.

So, when you quit drinking and come across all *goody two shoes the teetotaller* you subconsciously cause them pain. All human beings will respond to pain by trying to either move away from it or make it stop. Your friends and family are unlikely to disown you because you stopped drinking but whether they are conscious of it or not they may try to tempt you back into the alcohol fold, so that you are no longer causing them pain. Watch out for innocent statements such as 'surely you can have one drink' or 'come on don't be anti social, just have one'. I don't believe there is any maliciousness in this behaviour, most people are not even aware they are doing it. It is simply a truth that people prefer to take the path of least resistance and that means it is easier to persuade you to lower your standards rather than attempt to raise their own.

Expecting support from other drinkers in your pursuit of giving up alcohol is fruitless. Essentially if you lie down with dogs you will get up with fleas. I strongly advise you to try and be around people who share your goal or at least agree with your decision. Perhaps you have a few friends who also want to stop drinking, why not get together and support each other? However, if you are making this journey alone, you can find local support groups such as AA or even join my private Facebook page. The members of this hidden club are truly amazing people. I constantly amazed at just how much they reach out to help and encourage each other and share beautiful stories of how their lives have turned around since they stopped drinking. Membership is free, you can get more information from my website.

6. Take 100% responsibility

The world you experience might be the same as the world I experience but it is equally as possible that it is entirely unique to you. How do we know that when we both look at the color blue that it appears the same to both of us? This is your own personal universe; it's time to take responsibility for your creation and stop pointing the finger of blame and making excuses. How often have you decided to go on a diet but at the last minute opted to start on Monday rather than straight away. How often have you delayed taking action on your drinking until after summer, after Christmas, after the dog's birthday? Make a commitment that you will break that loop today.

Imagine you are floating on your back in a river, gently flowing with the water. Suddenly the water begins to start flowing faster and faster and you find yourself going over a waterfall. Having splashed awkwardly over the edge and recovered your composure you probably wouldn't start blaming the waterfall for what happened, you would not take it personally. But this is what we do with life, shit happens and our ego insists that it's personal. Most of the time it isn't and blame never solves anything.

The ego likes to stick labels on things:

- The new car in your drive = good thing
- The tax demand in your mail box = bad thing
- The vacation you have planned = good thing
- Your boss won't give you time off work = bad thing

Labels are actions of the ego and always come from a position of fear. They distract you from taking responsibility and encourage you to point the finger of blame. Most labels are an illusion because they are highly subjective. For example if you found $50 in the street you would probably label that event a good thing but it certainly wasn't for the person who lost it. They would label it a bad thing, the same event becomes both good and bad at the same time – so what is the point of a label. It is neither good nor bad, it just is!

So you have a drink problem, you can blame your stressful job, your genetics or even something as vague as 'your crappy luck' but it won't help you stop drinking. Accept responsibility for the problem you have, there is no need or point in labelling yourself as weak willed or any other negative description. Your alcohol problem is a waterfall in your river of life, it happened – so deal with it and move on.

7. Reprogram your subconscious

The final step in the 'Alcohol Escape Plan' is subconscious reprogramming. As we have discussed, all the issues we face in life are our responsibility, as they are manifested directly by us, via the programs that run in our subconscious mind. Most of these sub-routines are beneficial and serve a valuable purpose such as controlling our body temperature and keeping us breathing at the correct rate.

However, along our journey through this life we pick up the odd erroneous program that creates unhelpful manifestations. These 'bad programs' make us fat, create low self-esteem and even get us addicted to harmful substances.

Thankfully we are prevented by nature from lifting the hood on the subconscious mind and tinkering with the engine. Of course our ego would have us believe that we are master mechanics, fully capable of making perfect adjustments to this most powerful of computers. The subconscious knows better and the gate is kept firmly closed to the over zealous ego.

Using hypnosis we can bypass the conscious mind and implant positive corrections directly into the subconscious. As this part of the mind has no ability to judge or question, the implanted commands are run exactly as requested.

This section of the method is optional and many have stopped drinking completely without ever having used one of my hypnosis downloads. However, as with everything else I have told you so far. This was an important element for me and I want you to use every tool in the box to ensure we get the job done in one painless motion. If you do think these powerful audio tracks would help you then please stop by my website for the mp3 download details.

It is important that we ensure we fully understand what hypnosis is, or more importantly what it is not. Hypnosis is not black magic, a party trick nor a piece of theatre. It is a naturally occurring process of the brain that has unfortunately attracted some seriously bad press over recent years; some might say even OJ Simpson has had better press than hypnosis!

Thankfully, for over two thousand years it was documented and practiced with a great deal of respect. How bizarre that this long studied and amazing action of the human mind was essentially defamed by a man in a bar trying to convince girls to remove their clothes.

The traditional stage hypnotist is considered by most right thinking hypnotherapists and psychologists as a blundering incompetent dabbling in something they don't truly understand. If they did understand the amazing process they are playing with, I would suggest they would find something more productive to do with it than make a person believe they are a little fluffy duck called Roger!

A common misconception about hypnosis is that it is sleep. Although a hypnotized person appears to be sleeping, they are actually quite alert. Hypnosis is very difficult to describe, as nobody actually knows what is going on inside the mind of a subject. What we do know is that while in the trance state, the subject becomes very suggestible. A subject's attention, while they are going into trance, is narrowed down gradually.

Many areas of normal communication are removed one by one. Starting with sight, a person is asked to close his eyes and concentrate. Other senses are then removed from the equation;

some people even lose complete feeling of their body. That may sound frightening, but it is accomplished in a slow, pleasant way, rather than suddenly turning off of a switch.

You enter a world of hyper relaxation and at the same time hyper awareness. As you might expect, as you remove certain senses the remaining ones become more acute to compensate. Often people who have been under hypnosis will come around and claim, "it did not work". When you enquire as to why they believe hypnosis did not occur, they make statements such as "I could hear everything", "I could even hear the cars going past the window!" This is all part of the misconception that hypnosis is sleep, and that during trance you are unconscious, when in actual fact you are hyper conscious.

I am telling you about hypnosis not because I want you to take to the stage, but because I want you to understand the truly amazing power of the subconscious mind. A person in hypnosis is highly suggestible. The hypnotist has direct access to the person's subconscious without having to go through the conscious mind. This is how they can convince a six-foot tall, 250lb man he is a light gentle ballet dancer and have him pirouetting his way around the stage.

Hypnosis is so natural, that you do it dozens of times a day without even realizing it. Have you ever driven home at the end of your working day and arrived home with no memory of the journey? Hypnosis just paid you a visit, your brain was using the opportunity of this familiar and fairly simple task to filter and file information in your brain.

You may notice yourself at work blankly staring at the computer screen in a deep peaceful daydream. This happens due to the vast amount of information constantly entering your brain, every few hours your mind must pause a little to filter and file all the information you have learned. Placing it in the correct storage area of the brain.

For example, let's say in the last hour your brain has learned that the color of the walls in the canteen are yellow. It has also learnt that your new managers' name is David. It must ensure the information you will need on an ongoing basis is stored close to hand. Unfortunately this is at the expense of the canteen walls, and I am sorry to say, if questioned, you may have trouble remembering what color those walls were - but who cares, walls may have ears, but I have noticed they stay pretty dumb when asked for a pay rise!

In my online stop drinking club, I use hypnosis to further embed the six steps of my stop drinking method. I do this because I know that the conscious mind is a guard dog. The sort of animal the mail man must first distract before he opens the gate and creeps up the path to post the mail through the letterbox, after doing so he sneaks back out, hopefully without being noticed.

During this book I have been directly talking to your guard dog, you can choose to accept what I am saying, or dismiss it. During hypnosis you do not have that problem; all suggestions are accepted without judgment because the words are directed to the subconscious.

Don't lie there waiting for something magical to happen, don't expect or demand anything, you will also need to be prepared to catch your ego trying to pull you out of the moment. It's fine when it does, if you find your mind wandering just notice what has happened, smile and refocus on the now. Relax and let the music and my words drift over you. There is nothing that you can do wrong, free yourself of that concern and let go of all expectation.

Part of the fear of giving up drinking is that you might spend the rest of your life with an itch you can't scratch; Living in a permanent state of wanting a drink but not being able to touch it. This is not a cure; this is a torturous and constant battle with the ego that you can't possibly expect to win in the long term. Imagine being so at ease with alcohol that you can honestly say you don't want a drink, you don't like the taste of it, and if someone pushed a glass of it into your hand you would rather go out of your way to find a replacement than take the slightest sip. This state is possible, I know because I have been through the process I have just described to you, and now I live it everyday.

Thank you for reading The Alcohol Escape Plan with me, I sincerely hope it helps you take the first step out of this very destructive loop of alcohol addiction. When you get to the point where you can confidently claim that alcohol is no longer a part of your life I want to hear from you. Please contact me via the website and let me know just how many amazing things have appeared in your life since you got rid of the attractively packaged poison.

Remember, if you need a little extra help with this process then you can join my VIP mentoring program at www.StopDrinkingExpert.com

If you have enjoyed this book please would you go back to the online store where you bought it and leave a rating and review? This little act will take but a few minutes and it will really help get this valuable material to more people who desperately need it.

Websites:
www.CraigBeck.com
www.StopDrinkingExpert.com

Social Media
https://www.facebook.com/craigbeckbooks/
https://twitter.com/craigbeck

You Don't Have to Do It Alone…
Join the online coaching club that has helped over 100,000 people
just like you to get back in control of their drinking.

www.stopdrinkingexpert.com

Are you sick and tired of feeling sick and tired?

Maybe you are finding that more and more you are turning to alcohol on an evening to 'relax' and cope with life?

Perhaps you are dealing with serious health problems, financial worries and failing relationships. Plus the guilt of not giving the people you love the 'real you' anymore?

I understand how you feel!

First of all, you should know that I was a heavy drinker myself. Alcohol became something that I couldn't control despite how miserable it was making me.

I had an outstanding career, beautiful home and family but one by one alcoholism was destroying them all.

Every day I made excuses about why I 'needed' to drink.

All the time, failing to make the connection that my alcoholism was the reason for the vast majority of my problems.

- My health was going downhill fast
- My marriage was falling apart
- I was missing quality time with my children
- My career was going nowhere fast
- I was descending deeper and deeper into debt
- Depression, worry and unhappiness were my life

My drinking was hurting everyone I loved.

My family was everything to me! I would have defended and protected them with my life.

In contrast here I was, badly hurting them myself!

My nightly drinking had turned me into a fat, selfish zombie. I wasn't interested in anything but drinking.

It made me so selfish! As a result I wouldn't go anywhere or do anything unless I could drink at the same time. All clear signs of addiction but still I refused to accept it.

I am ashamed to admit I was a terrible husband and nowhere near the father I set out to be.

There was no way I was going to AA!

I wanted someone to show me how to stop drinking alcohol, but Alcoholics Anonymous was too depressing, also I had my professional reputation to think about. Consequently, I didn't want to stand up in a room full of strangers and label myself 'an alcoholic'.

Rehab was too expensive and I couldn't risk taking an extended leave from work!

I tried almost everything.

From silly gimmicks, herbal supplements and hypnosis through to prescription medication (recklessly ordered from abroad online). It seemed like nothing made any real difference.

Solution' Has Helped Over 100,000 Drinkers

How to stop drinking without all the usual struggle:
When I gave up trying to force myself to cut back. It was only then I discovered how to deal with my alcoholism in a more logical and simple way.

I changed the meaning of alcohol, it stopped being something a saw as a special treat. As a result it became something I saw as nothing more than 'attractively packaged poison'.

Finally, life suddenly became... peaceful, happy and secure.

I lost weight, slept like a baby, reconnected with my family, regained my career and even more.

It became so easy that the years I had struggled to force myself to cut back seemed silly.
I had tried hundreds of times to moderate my drinking. All the time dreaming of drinking like a 'normal' person.

Creating silly rules for myself:

- I told myself I would only drink beer, never wine (FAILED)
- Then I promised I would only drink on special occasions (FAILED)
- I said I would quit drinking at home and only drink socially (FAILED)
- Yet, In all other areas of my life I was successful.

Nobody outside my close family had any idea I was knocking back two bottles of wine a night, every night.

My friends just thought I could 'handle my drink', like it was something to be proud of!

Then I Had A Lightbulb Moment!

Everyone claims that quitting drinking is difficult, miserable and painful right?

The reason is because drinkers the world over are using the same broken 'solution' over and over and expecting the outcome to change.

Trying to force yourself to moderate your drinking has a 95% chance of failure.

So why then does EVERY traditional way of dealing with alcohol addiction still uses this as the 'go to solution'?

Perhaps willpower does not work?

Twelve-step programs tell you that you are broken and always will be

Consequently, you must spend the rest of your life forcing yourself to stay away from the thing you want the most!

Likewise, rehab costs tens of thousands of dollars to do exactly the same thing.

Using prescription medication to deal with any addiction still requires willpower in order to keep taking the tablets.

Plus they come with side-effects worse than a hangover!

Absolutely no judgment or embarrassment - Deal with this entirely in the privacy of your own home.

If it wasn't killing over three million people every year (according to World Health Organization figures) it might even be funny.

But for those of us trapped in the loop, it's not funny. It's a miserable experience.

Therefore, these days I devote my time to showing people how to stop drinking alcohol in a rather more simple way. No embarrassing group meetings, no expensive rehab, no dangerous medications and absolutely zero ineffective willpower.

Your health is going to get dramatically better
Within 3 months of quitting drinking my high blood pressure vanished. More than that, it return to perfectly normal levels, despite being elevated for over a decade.

My sleep apnea cleared up and the scary pain in my side went away and never came back. Therefore, proving to me once and for all that it was being caused by my drinking all along.

Who knows what would have happened if I had carried on drinking.

I lost 57lbs of body fat without any real effort. It turns out there is a lot of calories in all that alcohol I was knocking back.

But my story is not unique. You are about to find out for yourself the significant health benefits of kicking the attractively packaged poison out of your life:

1. Better quality sleep.
2. More energy.
3. Clarity and less brain fog.
4. Clearer skin.
5. Increased mental focus.
6. Effortless weight loss.
7. Improved blood pressure.
8. Reduced risk of cancer.
9. Better immune system.
10. Improved memory function.

Your relationships will get so much better
If you are a problem drinker your relationships are under an unbearable amount of pressure.

The hard truth is, drinkers are focused on when they can have their next drink. As a result they don't spend a lot of time considering how they can be a loving, caring and passionate husband or wife.

When you learn how to stop drinking alcohol using my method, so many good things happen to your relationships:

1. No more drunken arguments and saying things you will regret.
2. More quality time together.
3. Never choosing alcohol over your partner again.
4. Sexual dysfunction and impotence can improve.

5. More passionate and enjoyable sex where you are both 100% present.
6. Stop giving your partner the 'lazy zombie' version of the person they met.
7. Be the loving, attentive parent that you set out to be.
8. Rediscover the authentic you.

Plus: The average member saves thousands... every year

The average member saves over $6000 per year. But alcohol is stealing so much more than the financial cost!

When you're sober, you naturally operate at your maximum capacity. You're lucid, focused, and you wake up feeling like a million bucks every day (this benefit cannot be overstated).

When I was drinking, my effectiveness on any given day might have been around 80%.

Now, I feel like I'm constantly operating at 98% or more. What's incredible is that this improvement has had an exponential impact on the tangible success I've achieved.

Get back in control of your life easily with this course

I always dreamed of escaping the rat race and being my own boss. For over a decade my drinking problem prevented me from even getting started.

As soon as I discovered how to stop drinking alcohol for good, my life started to change in the most amazing ways.

I quit drinking and then I quit my miserable 9 to 5 job. Today, I never go to 'the office', likewise, I am never stuck in the dreaded commute and I don't have a boss to answer to.

Thousands of people just like you have done exactly the same thing with my help...

Just as soon as they kick this life limiting poison out of their lives for good.

Decide now & be the next to quit drinking without any of the usual hard work or struggle.

FREE QUIT DRINKING WEBINAR
RESERVE YOUR PLACE NOW
www.StopDrinkingExpert.com

Sign up for my next free quit drinking webinar and I will personally take you through the easy, step by step process:

1. How to escape problem drinking safely, quickly & easily
2. Dealing with your drinking friends and family
3. Relaxing without a drink
4. Dealing with stress and anxiety
5. Destroy all cravings in 3 easy moves
6. Sleep better and rest better
7. How to vacation & celebrate without alcohol (and have a great time)
8. Retaking control of life and going after your dreams.

I understand where you currently are. I was a heavy drinker myself (for nearly two decades). Alcohol became something that I couldn't control despite how miserable it was making me.

I had a great job, beautiful home and family but... one by one alcoholism stole them all from me. Every day I made excuses about why I 'needed' to drink. All the time, I failed to make the connection that my alcohol use was the reason for the vast majority of my problems.

AA was too depressing, and I didn't want to label myself as an alcoholic. Rehab was too expensive for my joyless and broke self. **Finally,** I realized willpower was not the answer to control my alcohol intake.

For nearly a decade I'd been fighting a losing battle!

When I eventually landed on a more logical method **of controlling my cravings for alcohol** without willpower or withdrawal. Life suddenly became peaceful and secure. I lost weight, slept like a baby, reconnected with my family, and regained my career.

Now I take this knowledge around the world with my highly respected Quit Drinking Bootcamp.

What to expect from Quit Drinking Bootcamp

- The Live quit drinking events are always small, friendly & non-judgmental. There will be no more than 20 people attending. Everyone in the room is in the same situation.
- You will not have to stand up (AA style) and label yourself an alcoholic (or anything at all). You can be as actively or passively involved as you want.
- The event is 100% private, confidential, and discreet. There will be no mention of alcohol on your card statement or anywhere at the venue.
- Dress comfortably, grab a coffee, and turn up at least ten minutes before the start time. Craig will take it from there. Take notes if you want, but it's not essential.
- The days run roughly 10 am to 4.30pm. There will be several comfort breaks and a chance to take a breather and grab some lunch.
- There is nothing further to buy, no up-selling & no need to attend any additional seminars. The event works in one day by deconstructing the foundations of why you turn to alcohol.

- There is no pressure to do anything. You don't even have to commit to stop drinking altogether - that will always be your choice.
- <u>Come along sober</u>, optimistic, and with an open mind. Follow the steps, and you will be able to quit drinking easily, painlessly, and without willpower.

For dates and ticket information visit
www.StopDrinkingExpert.com/quit-drinking-bootcamp/

CPSIA information can be obtained
at www.ICGtesting.com
Printed in the USA
BVHW031023110620
581297BV00020B/163